# Stitch TOKYO

Original title *Tokio sobre tela*, published by Editorial GG, Barcelona, Spain, 2024

First published in the United Kingdom in 2026 by
Batsford
43 Great Ormond Street
London WC1N 3HZ
An imprint of B. T. Batsford Holdings Limited



This edition is published by arrangement with Editorial GG



ISBN 978 1 83733 039 3

A CIP catalogue record for this book is available from the British Library.

10 9 8 7 6 5 4 3 2 1

Reproduction by Rival Colour Ltd., UK
Printed and bound by Dream Colour, China

This book can be ordered direct from the publisher at www.batsfordbooks.com, or try your local bookshop

Distributed throughout the UK and Europe by Abrams & Chronicle Books, 1st Floor, 22–24 Ely Place, London EC1N 6TE and 57 rue Gaston Tessier, 75166 Paris, France

www.abramsandchronicle.co.uk
info@abramsandchronicle.co.uk

# Stitch TOKYO

BATSFORD

OCEAN BOMB
COFFEE
BOSS
HOT
KIRIN

# CONTENTS

# KON NICHI WA!

## I'm so glad you picked up this book!

I've written it with Japanese culture lovers in mind; those who smile when they remember a little street in a Tokyo neighbourhood; who feel joy when they hear the song of the metro; whose mouths water on seeing a bowl of ramen...

This is no ordinary embroidery book. In its pages, you will find a fusion of my two passions: embroidery and Japan. I hope that the techniques and tricks I share with you will inspire you to create unique and imaginative pieces.

GAMBARE!

TOKU-CHAN
Nurge No 2

# WABI-SABI

**The phrase 'wabi-sabi' refers to finding beauty in imperfection. This conveys the idea that true beauty lies in the simplest of things, regardless of their flaws.**

This is precisely what I experience when I'm in Japan: I see beauty everywhere, and an endless array of places and objects perfect for recreating through embroidery.

You don't need to know everything to feel inspired. You simply need to understand what you like and what makes you happy, and find a way to translate this into the language of thread. Focusing on this will test your ingenuity, as well as your desire to create something different using new techniques and textures.

My purpose with this book is to showcase various embroidery projects that incorporate three-dimensional elements and provide inspiration for new techniques.

大入

Cat Cafe
Pet Shop
16TAPI

営業中
中華食堂
一番館
ICHI-BAN-KAN
営業時間 11:00～24:00
つけ麺
546円
焼肉スタミナ炒飯
619円

しょしょ
証城寺
証城寺の
庭は
……

舞妓はん
ひぃ～ひぃ～
世界一辛い
七味

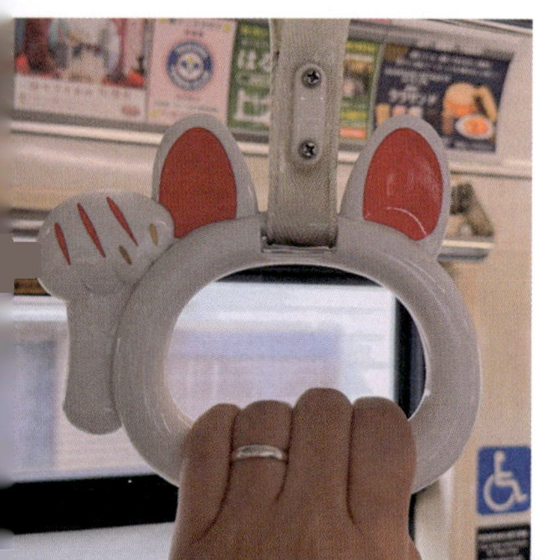

一八
そば
うどん

# GET INSPIRED AND CREATE SOMETHING

**Japan is an endless source of inspiration for me: vending machines, boxes of sweets, restaurant signs, the presentation of a bowl of ramen… I could go on!**

I take pictures of absolutely everything, and when I say 'everything', I mean everything! Even a restroom sign in a restaurant can be so amusing that I end up embroidering it onto a T-shirt.

One thing that's for certain is that I often improvise when I embroider. As a result, my projects can end up looking very different from what was originally planned. For instance, I might add a non-existent flower shop into the premises of my design simply because it looks prettier with a range of green hues.

I love all the real photos of Japan, but I have the most fun when creating an aesthetically pleasing appearance – or, in other words, making everything pretty. I tend to play with a range of warm colours to achieve this, as well as pinks, lilacs or pastel tones.

I usually edit my travel photographs using a graphics tablet, which allows me to design and paint them according to my preferred colour palette. I also decide whether to add highlights or beads at this stage.

It's equally important to take the foundation we're going to work on and what the final piece will look like into account. Should we use a frame or a canvas? Should it be wooden or plastic? Should we stick to the frame's natural colour or paint it? These small details all contribute to the finished piece and influence the final result.

# TOOLS AND MATERIALS

**Listed below are the basic tools and materials that I usually use, and that you will need to make the pieces in this book.**

## TOOLS

### EMBROIDERY HOOPS (FRAMES)

I always recommend Nurge embroidery hoops. They are made of high-quality beechwood, come in various sizes and, very importantly, hold the hoop taut so that you don't lose tension in the fabric while embroidering. They also make some plastic hoops in different shapes and colours, which are useful as you can work with them comfortably and also use them for framing.

### NEEDLES

I usually work with several needles of different thicknesses at the same time. The more threads you use, the larger the needle head required.

For single-strand detailing, I use Clover's Black Gold needles, which are very small and fine. For thicker threads, such as Colbert wool, I either use wool needles or Clover needles, which are high quality and can withstand long periods of use.

For felting, I use Clover's felting needles, which allow you to work with small or delicate materials using one, two or three needles.

### NEEDLE THREADER

I don't usually use a needle threader with multi-strand *mouliné* thread, but it's a lifesaver when adding single-strand details with fine needles. It allows me to thread needles in two seconds without breaking my rhythm. I always carry the Clover needle threader with me.

### SCISSORS

It's really important not to use the same scissors for everything. Fabric scissors are usually long and leave clean cuts in the fabric.

Thread scissors tend to be much smaller and easy to manoeuvre. They should always be sharp to make precise cuts in the thread.

### FABRIC PENS

Heat erasable pens are my favourite as they allow me to avoid getting my embroidery wet unless absolutely necessary. Pilot Frixion pens are quick and easy to use, and the ink disappears when ironed or heated with a hair dryer. I always have them in several colours. I usually use one for the design and another for making additional markings as I work.

There are many different types of heat erasable pens with various nib sizes. The fine-tipped ones make it easier to draw details, and there are also white ones for dark fabrics. My favourite brand, and the one I always have to hand, is Clover.

ベビースター

Heat transfer pencils are the best option for transferring designs onto difficult fabrics such as felt. Simply draw your design on a piece of paper and then run an iron over it to transfer the design to the fabric.

### PLIERS

You will need a pair of pliers to cut wire for stumpwork (see page 20).

## MATERIALS

### FABRICS

In general, I work with plain, unpatterned 100% cotton fabrics. Stretch fabrics can become distorted when placed in an embroidery hoop and may become wrinkled or produce an unintended result once removed. Cotton is my favourite fabric, without a doubt. I can print patterns on it, draw on it by hand and even paint it with watercolours without any issues.

I also tend to use felt in many of my pieces. Depending on the finish I'm looking for, I'll choose one type or the other. 100% wool felt has a rough appearance and doesn't change size, making it ideal for use as a base. On the other hand, felt containing viscose has a softer appearance, so I usually use this for more delicate projects.

I also use organza and tulle fabrics, which are ideal for creating certain effects as they are light and low-density.

Finally, for some projects, it can be useful to work with water-soluble fabric, which is made from materials that dissolve in water. These fabrics have an adhesive interlining that helps to make it more rigid.

## THREADS

*Mouliné* embroidery thread is the most popular and cheapest type you can find. Consisting of six separate strands, you can stitch with all six for a textured look, or you can use fewer strands for finer, more detailed work. All-purpose thread is a finer type of cotton *mouliné* with only one strand, which is great for very delicate details.

Other non-cotton threads are also available, such as metallic, iridescent and Colbert wool threads. While these are more delicate to work with, they produce an incredible finish.

## WOOL ROVING

Wool roving is used for felting. Using good materials is important to achieve a pretty finish and, in my experience, Clover natural wool roving is the best for this; it's perfectly combed, easy to use and produces excellent results.

If you use synthetic or low-quality wool roving, the finished product won't look smooth and polished. Instead, it will look scruffy and detract from the skill that went into the work.

## WATERCOLOURS

I use White Nights watercolours and have created a customized palette of my favourite colours. However, you can use any other brand you feel comfortable with.

## LEDs

Strips of micro LEDs have been available in most craft shops for some time now. I use this type of lighting in my work because they are malleable and easy to use.

## WIRE

I usually use fine 0.4 mm wire for jewellery or costume jewellery. Look for coated or rust-resistant wire to prevent corrosion over time.

## BEADS

I have a box full of different beads, made from minerals, plastics, Swarovski crystals... Any bead can add a unique touch to your work when you least expect it.

## GLUE

You will need textile glue to add details to your piece; any type will do.

**THREADS**

perlé

mouliné

étoile

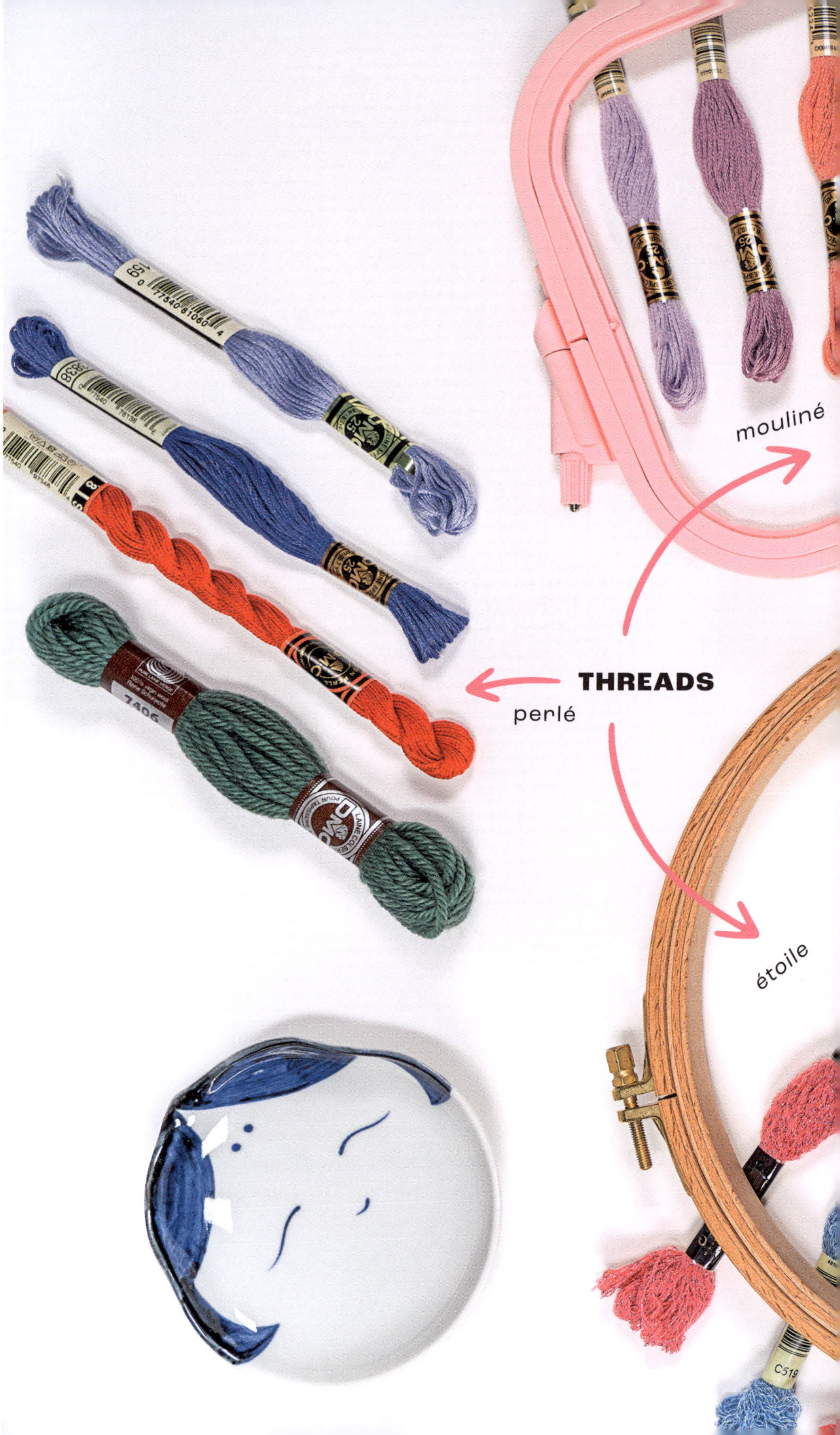

Metallic
THREAD
EMBROIDERY
HOOPS
WOOL ROVING
EMBROIDERY
SCISSORS
PLIERS
NATURAL WOOL ROVING
LAINE MÈCHE À FEUTRER
LANA NATURAL EN MECHA
NATUR-FILZWOLLE
Clover
NEEDLE
THREADER
Thread Slot
All purpose
THREAD

# TOOLS and MATERIALS

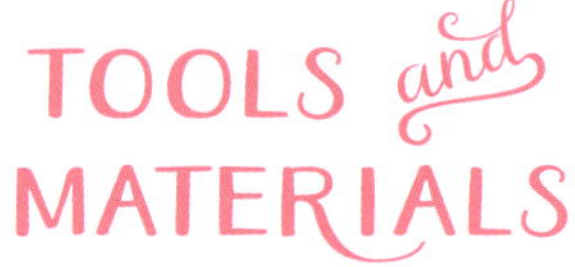

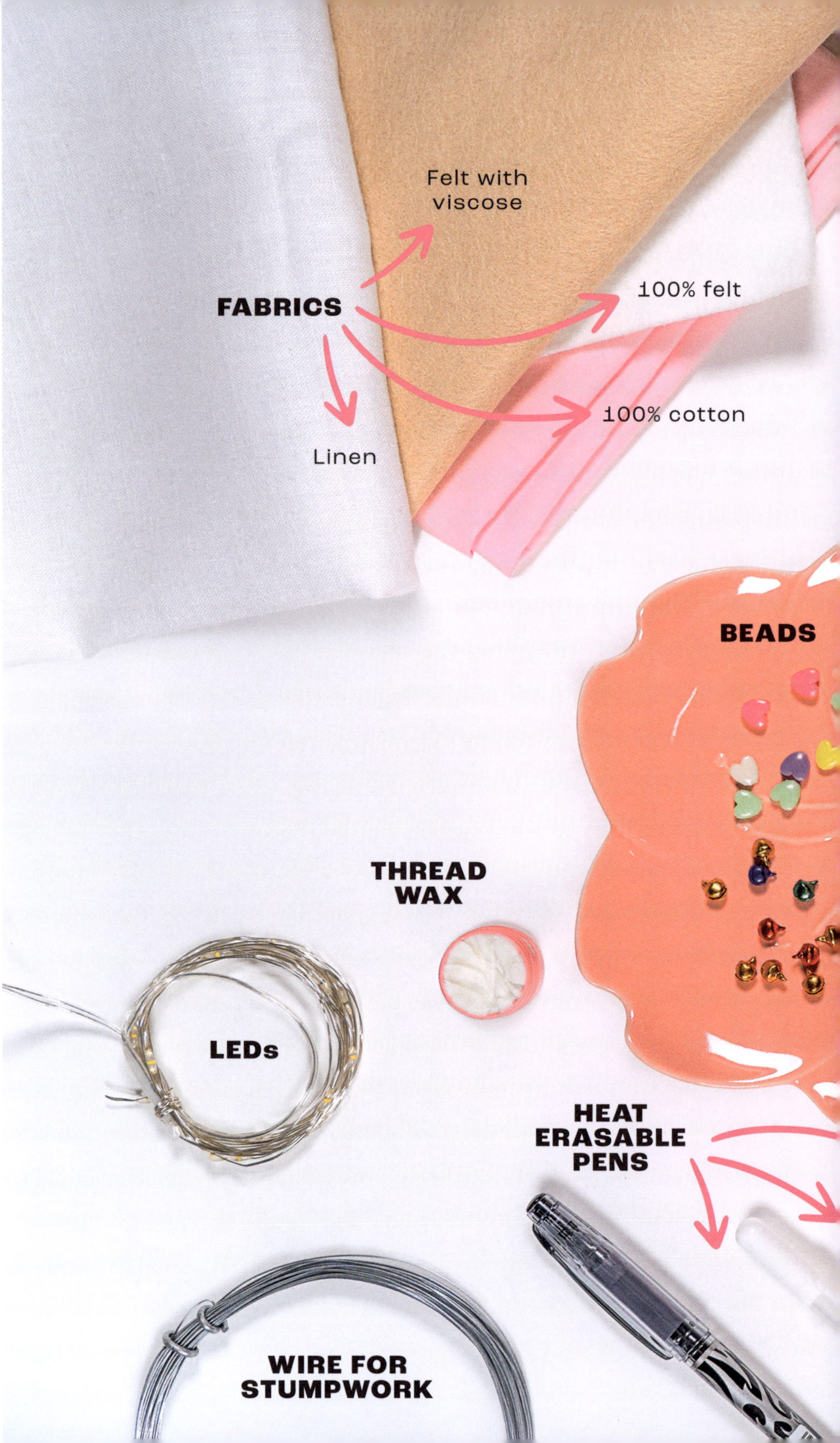
FABRICS
Felt with viscose
100% felt
100% cotton
Linen
BEADS
THREAD WAX
LEDs
HEAT ERASABLE PENS
WIRE FOR STUMPWORK

CUTTING PLIERS
FELTING NEEDLE
EMBROIDERY NEEDLES
For fabric
For thread
SCISSORS
TEXTILE GLUE
WATERCOLOURS
Heat transfer pencil

# THE BASICS OF EMBROIDERY

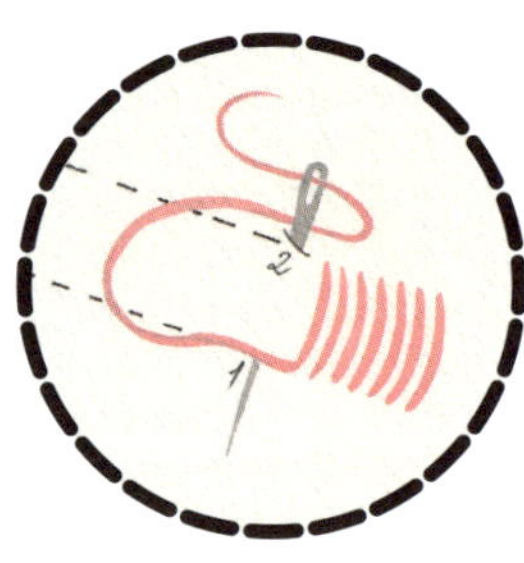

### ① SATIN STITCH

The satin stitch is ideal for adding large areas of colour or filling to your embroidery.

The process involves inserting the needle into the fabric and pulling it out at the other end with each turn. Place the stitches close together to create an even space in the middle and make sure that the thread doesn't curl up; the stitch should lie flat to achieve a smooth, seamless finish.

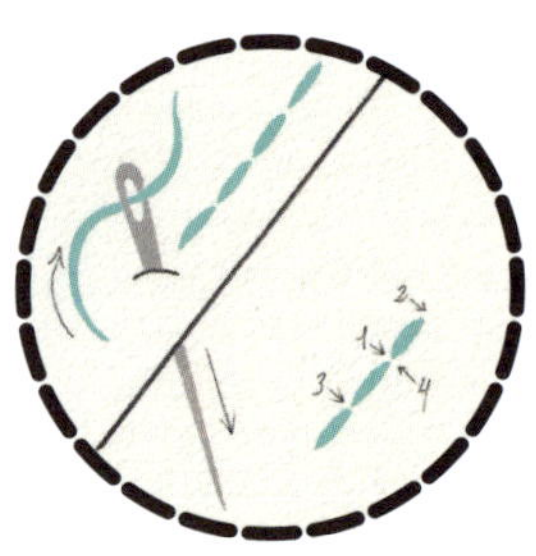

### ② BACK STITCH

This is my favourite stitch for outlining my pieces as it sharpens the edges of the embroidery. This technique uses short reverse stitches.

### ③ FRENCH KNOT

This stitch creates a tiny knot on the fabric. I love using this technique to add texture and volume to the embroidery.

To do this, pull the needle out and wrap the thread around it two or three times. Then, change the direction of the needle and insert it right next to where you pulled the needle through initially, keeping the thread taut with your other hand.

### STUMPWORK

Stumpwork is a technique used in embroidery to create three-dimensional elements or areas, by using specific materials and methods. These methods may involve working with silk or precious metals, using relief stitches, beading, quilting or wire.

This book will teach you how to incorporate these materials and techniques into your own embroidery projects, enabling you to create unique and original pieces of art.

①
③
STUMPWORK
②

1
2

# PREPARING THE FABRIC

**I usually work on my embroidery in hoops larger than the final size of the piece, as I like the embroidery to come out from inside the hoop once finished.**

For example, if the design I'm going to embroider is around 20cm (8in), I'll use a hoop of roughly 25cm (10in).

Before I start embroidering, I check that the fabric is completely taut in the hoop. To achieve this, I lightly secure the fabric between the two hoops before tightening the screw and pulling it several times (2). You'll know the fabric is ready to work on when it sounds like a drum upon gently tapping it with your finger (3).

I also use this time beforehand to do some colour testing with the watercolours and to make sure that I have all the needles required for the project to hand.

# TRANSFERRING DESIGNS TO FABRIC

**There are several methods to transfer your designs to fabric. These are the methods that I normally use and find to be the most effective.**

First, by hand: I usually transfer designs by hand for very large pieces, or pieces without much detail. The second method is to use a printer, which is definitely my favourite method when designing buildings with lots of straight lines, as it ensures that none of them get twisted.

#### TRANSFERRING BY HAND

One option is to print the design to size, stick it to the back of the fabric in the frame (1), place it against a window or on a light box (2) and trace it with a heat erasable pen (3).

You can also open the design on your computer or graphics tablet to the desired size, place the fabric (again, already in the frame) on top of the screen and trace it directly.

**TRANSFERRING WITH A PRINTER**

To use a printer, you will need adhesive foils, which you can buy in most stationery shops. Stick the foil onto the fabric that you are going to embroider (1, 2, 3), trim off any excess around the edges so that it doesn't get stuck in the printer (4), then insert it into the foil tray and print the design.

I usually iron the fabric beforehand to remove any wrinkles that could affect the print quality or attract dirt from the printer. It's also important to make sure that the print heads and output trays are clean, to prevent them from staining the fabric.

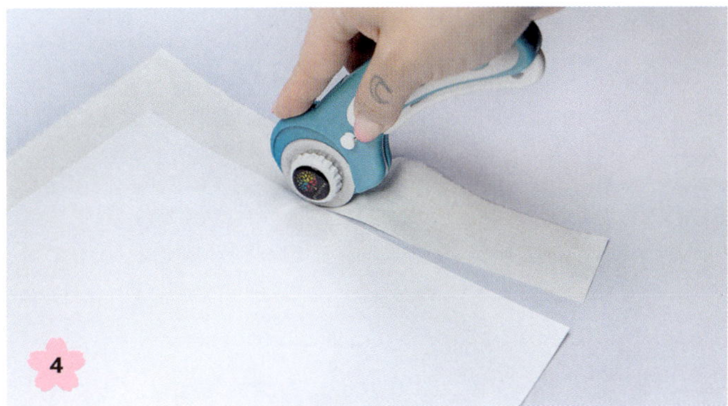

# FINAL TOUCHES

**Embroidered fabrics usually slacken in the frame over time. To combat this, as soon as I have finished a piece, I secure it with a thread at the back. This means that when the fabric loosens, I only have to cut the threads, re-tighten the fabric and sew it back together.**

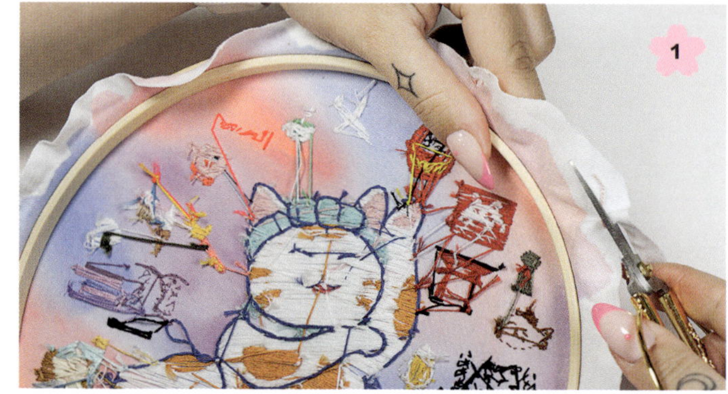


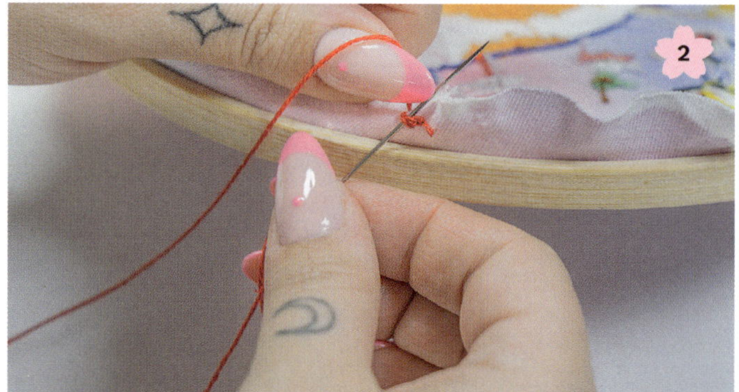

First, I cut off any excess fabric around the hoop (1), leaving a margin of about 1–2cm (roughly ½in). I then tie a knot on one side of the fabric (2) and make several stitches around the hoop (3). As I pull the thread, the fabric tightens within the hoop. To remove any stubborn bumps and pull the fabric taut, I use the same thread to make long stitches from end to end (4).

This way, you can hang your embroidery on a wall or display it in a frame. There are many ways you can show off your embroidery; depending on the design, I like to put it in a frame with a nice background and place an object inside with it. This method also helps to protect it from dust.

NEXT STATION
Mister Donut
Milky
TOKYO MAP
JR
JR東日本
大英堂製パン店
TEL (322) 0611
TAKESHITA St.
WEGO
CAT CAFE
YOSHINOYA
1F.
PUCK

maidreamin
SEGA
SEGA
Sweets Hotel RUBY

# TAIYAKI pincushion

**I fell in love with *taiyaki* the moment I saw it, before I even knew what it was. Then, when I tried it in Japan, I fell even more in love with it.**

It's a delicious, fish-shaped sponge cake filled with anko (sweet red bean paste) or matcha, which is cooked on cast iron plates right in front of you.

I miss *taiyaki* so much that I decided to make myself a very plump taiyaki pincushion that I always have on display while I work.

### YOU WILL NEED:

- Felt viscose blend fabric
- DMC *coton perlé* thread
- Needles
- Embroidery hoop
- Heat transfer pencil
- Cotton or cushion stuffing

**Stencil on page 113**

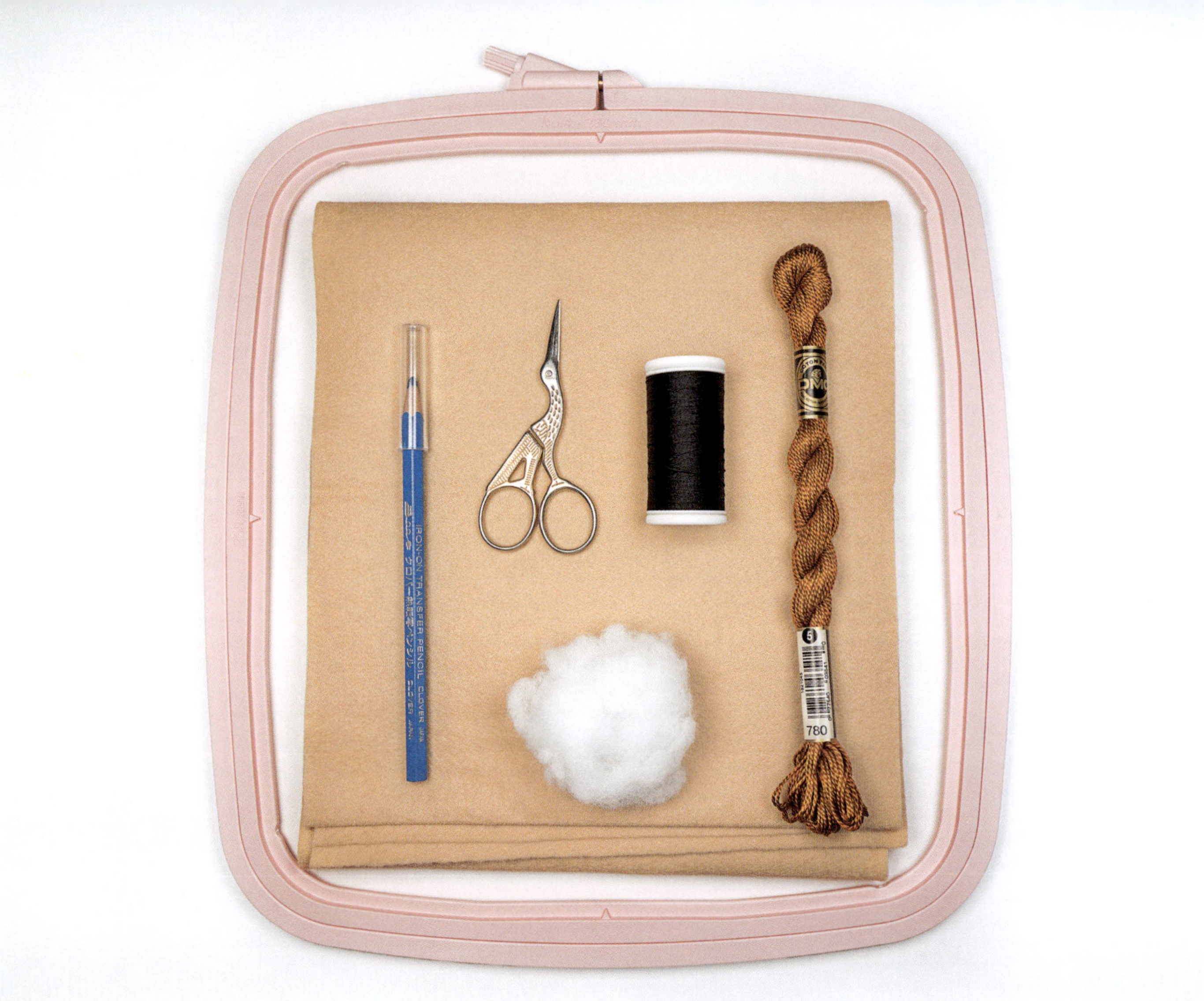
IRON-ON TRANSFER PENCIL CLOVER
DMC
780

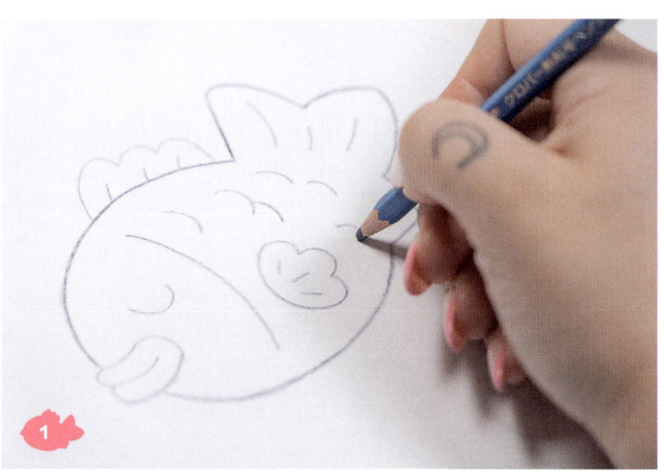

1

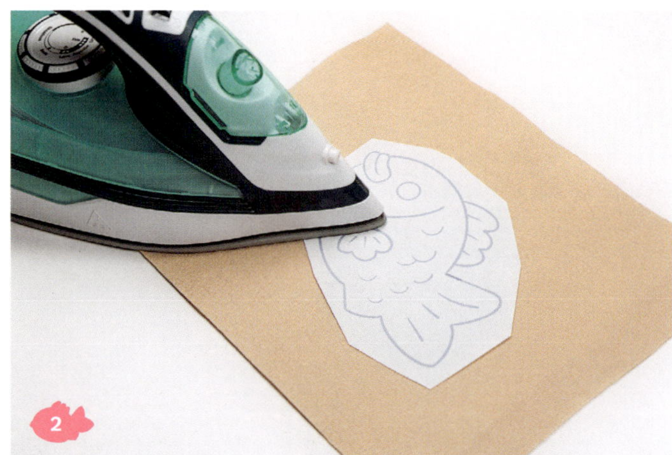

2

With a heat transfer pencil, trace the *taiyaki* design on page 113 onto a sheet of paper (1).

Stick the sheet onto the felt and iron to transfer the design (2).

Secure the felt in the frame, making sure that it remains taut (3).

Embroider the inner lines with short back stitches, using *perlé* thread in a darker shade than the felt (4). Leave the outline and lines of the fin to the end.

Once you have made the stitches on both sides of the *taiyaki*, use a pencil to mark the outline of each side, leaving a margin of 1cm (⅖in) before cutting them out (5, 6).

Line up both sides so that they are even and secure them with a few long stitches around the perimeter (7).

Embroider the outline, bringing the two sides close together but leaving enough space to insert the stuffing (8).

Insert the stuffing into the *taiyaki* and stitch up the opening so that it's closed (9, 10).

Use the scissors to tidy up the outline (11).

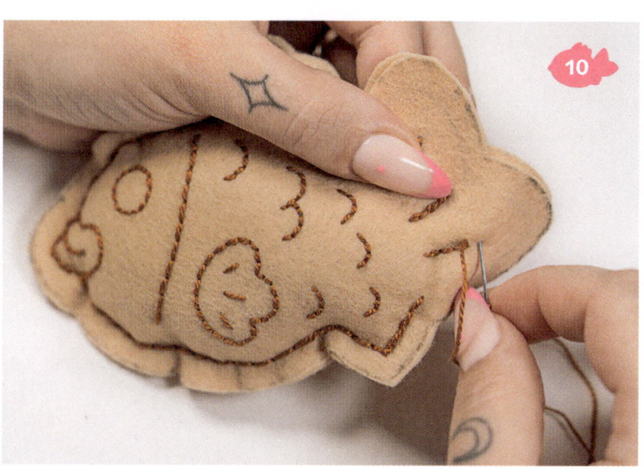

**Once fully stuffed, embroider the rest of the body and fins so that they stick together.**

RAMEN
brooch

## Take me anywhere there's good ramen!

Ramen is, without a doubt, one of my favourite foods. The flavours and ingredients can vary slightly, so I like to try them all. But the thing I love most about ramen is how beautifully it is presented.

To make our ramen brooch, you only need a few 'ingredients': thread, felt, skewers and not much else!

## YOU WILL NEED:

- Felt fabric
- Adhesive interlining fabric
- DMC *coton perlé* thread
- Needles
- Embroidery hoop
- Heat erasable pen
- Skewers
- Textile glue
- Two brooches (with pins)
- One gold-plated steel chain

**Stencil on page 114**

Iron some thick adhesive interlining fabric under the felt to stiffen the brooch (1).

Place the felt into the hoop and draw all the ramen ingredients onto it. Once you have done this, embroider them using short back stitches (2).

For the details, use a single strand of thread in a Naruto-style pink (3).

With black thread, mark the perimeter of the bowl and the black border using back stitches (4).

5
6
7
8
9
10

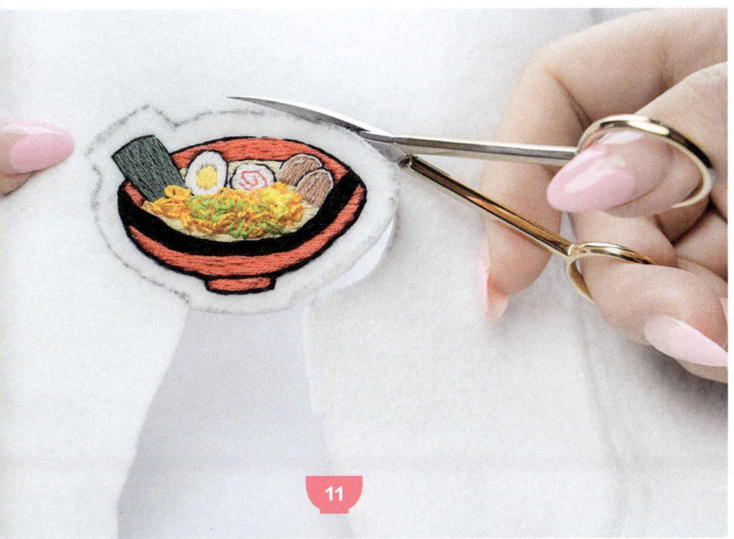

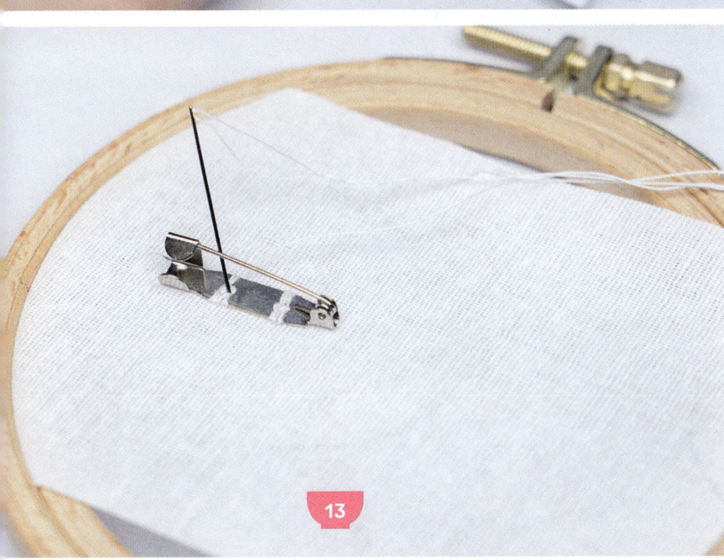


To create the noodles, use *perlé* thread and stitch without going all the way through the fabric. This will leave small loops that give the noodles more volume (5). Make more ingredients with other loose stitches and French knots (6, 7).

Cut two skewer sticks and file the ends a little to avoid splinters, then glue them to the felt with textile glue (8). For a better hold, and also for a little decoration, stitch a few loops at the top (9).

Outline and cut out the ramen and chopsticks, leaving a 0.5cm (2⁄5in) border of fabric (10, 11).

Mark the perimeter of the ramen and chopsticks on another piece of stiff adhesive interlining fabric (12). Then, place this on the frame and sew the back of the brooches on with a needle (13).

Cut the backs out and glue them to the chopsticks and ramen. Then, using small stitches in the felt, connect the two brooches with a gold-plated steel chain (14). It will look as if your chopsticks are picking up the ramen noodles!

ITADAKIMASU!

# SHINJUKU 3D CAT

**One of my favourite haberdasheries can be found in the Shinjuku district. I have often wandered through its streets, where it's impossible not to hear cats meowing songs in the distance. Yes, you read that right – meowing songs!**

At the main crossroads in Shinjuku, in front of the JR train station, they have installed a giant curved screen that displays a gorgeous 3D cat. The cat meows, plays and lowers its head as if watching the people passing by. Sometimes it even sings into a microphone!

When I was there, everyone was smiling and taking pictures of it. I thought to myself, 'I have to make this.'

## YOU WILL NEED:

- **Felt fabric**
- **Adhesive interlining fabric**
- **DMC *coton perlé* thread**
- **Clover natural wool roving**
- **Needles**
- **Felting needle**
- **Embroidery hoop**
- **Heat erasable pen**
- **Textile glue**
- **Beads**

**Stencil on page 115**

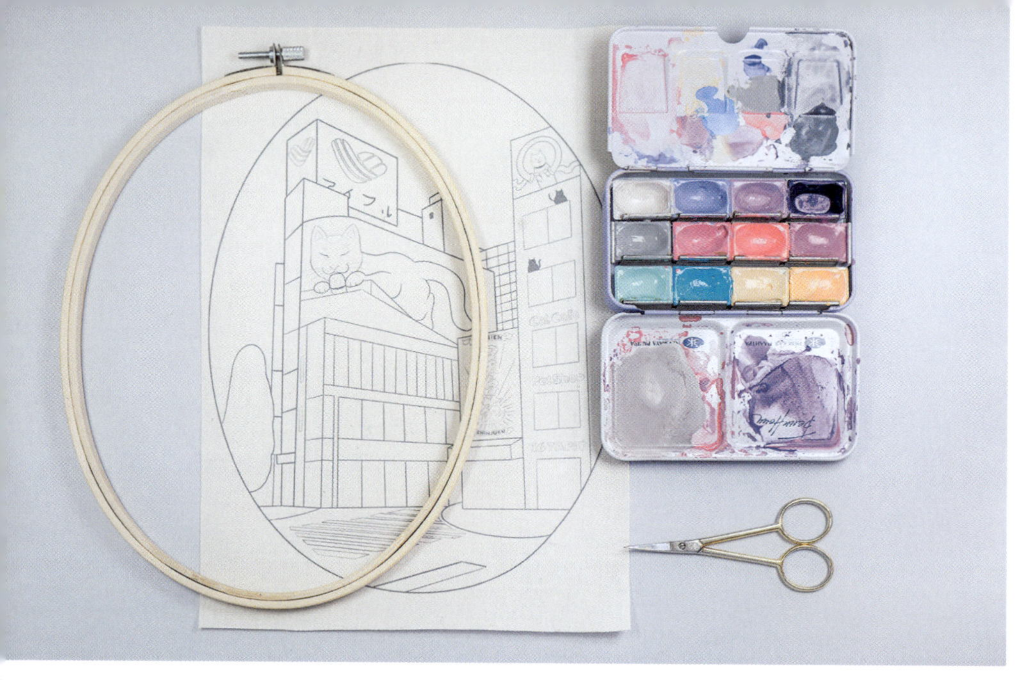

**Whenever I make buildings with lots of windows, I always follow this strict order, which I think is essential for achieving a good result.**

1

Once you have added the pattern to your fabric, study the design carefully and start by painting the skies, or any areas you want to be flat (1).

Use a heat erasable pen to make small marks on the edge of the window lines (2).

Start embroidering the inside of the window using satin stitches.

Then, with a single strand of thread, sew along the lines where you marked the windows (3, 4). Start with the longest lines, then the shortest, to hold the threads in place.

Work on the outlines last, so that these stitches stand out the most (5, 6).

**Add the beads at the end to prevent them getting caught in the threads and damaging the piece while you are embroidering.**

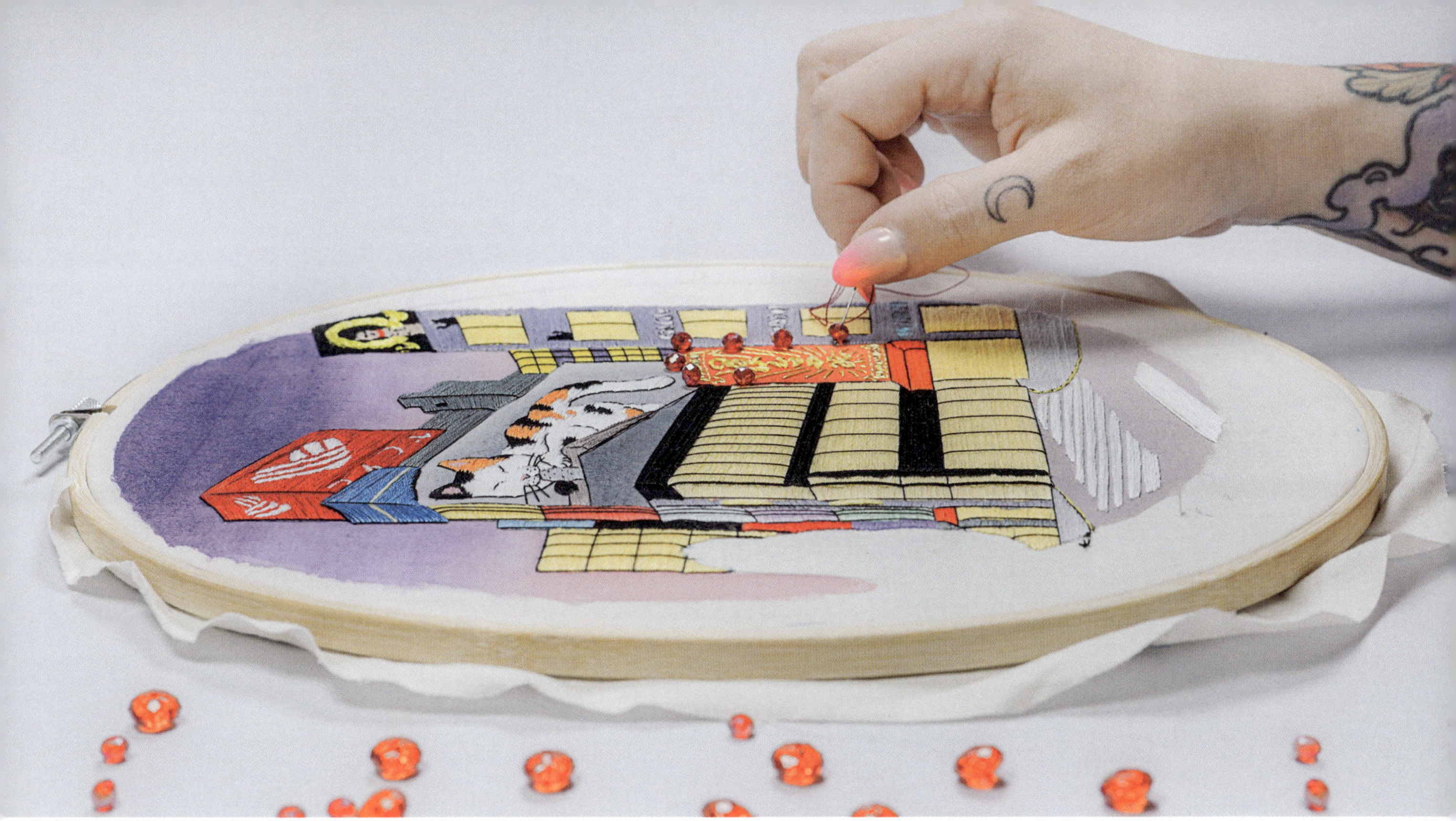

# SWEETS HOTEL

## Love Hotels in Japan are often very unique, with interiors inspired by anime themes, karaoke or arcades.

I had heard about the Sweets Hotel Ruby, a hotel where both the front of the building and its interior were covered in giant sweets. After doing some research, I discovered that it was located in a hidden alleyway very close to Shibuya JR Station.

There are two premises – one pink and the other chocolate brown. Obviously, the pink one is my favourite.

The buttons and sweet-shaped beads I found on the internet determined the final size of this piece, so that everything would be to scale.

### YOU WILL NEED:

- Cotton fabric
- DMC *mouliné* thread
- Needles
- Embroidery hoop
- Heat transfer pencil
- Beads or pink sweet-shaped buttons (or similar)

**Stencil on page 116**

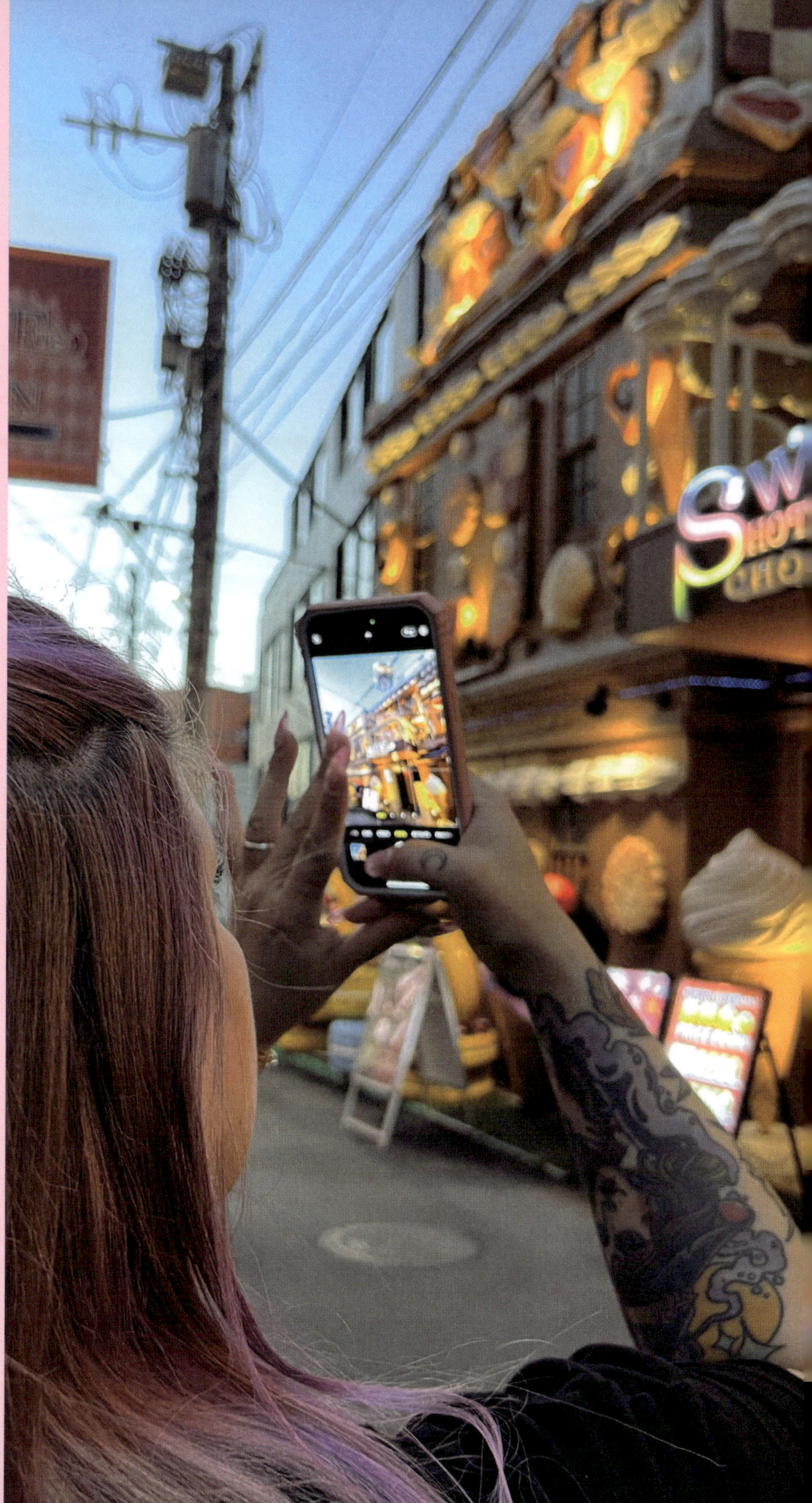

# Transfer the design to your fabric.

Paint the sky using watercolours.

Embroider the shapes with satin stitches.

Outline the edges with long stitches.

Add the beads and buttons using a single thread, taking care not to damage the embroidery.

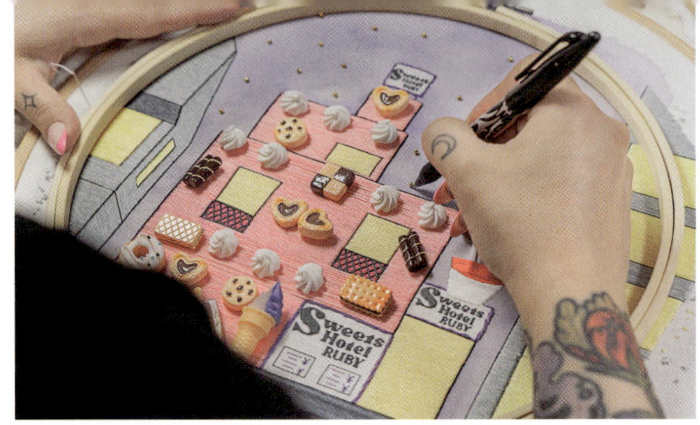

Sweets
Hotel
RUBY

集
消
火
栓

# MANHOLE covers

**In Japan, many of the manhole covers, or *manhoru*, have unique designs. These designs are often inspired by animal and plant species from different regions, typical foods, historical events or even famous manga and anime characters.**

For this project, I decided to create a fireman *manhoru*. To achieve the 3D appearance of these manhole covers, I worked with watercolours and full *mouliné* threads. I try to use watercolours wherever possible as they really help to add volume to the embroidery.

**YOU WILL NEED:**

- Cotton fabric
- DMC *mouliné* thread
- Needles
- Embroidery hoop
- Heat transfer pencil

**Stencil on page 117**

Paint the fabric background with yellow watercolour paint. It is important to remember to paint the fabric before embroidering when working with watercolours, otherwise the paint may stain the thread.

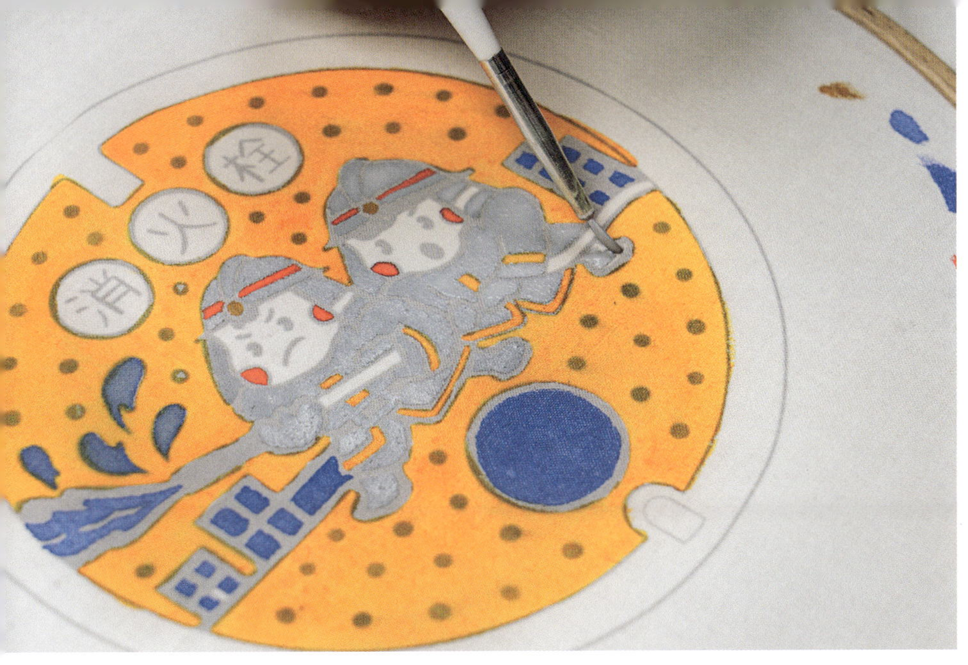

**Using six-strand *mouliné* thread, stitch the lines of the manhole cover with short back stitches.**

# GYOZA TIGER

## It doesn't matter what the gyozas are filled with... if the dough is homemade, I won't even leave the plate on the table!

Whenever I can, I cook gyozas at home. One day, while I was filling a homemade one, I thought to myself, 'This would be really cool embroidered'... And that thought stayed with me until my last trip to Tokyo.

While exploring the Asakusa district, I came across the Gyoza Tiger restaurant. I was drawn to it, quite frankly, because of the tiger logo on the door. My mouth started to water as I read the menu with its wide variety of gyozas and we chose to eat there, no questions asked.

Between the logo, the delicious food and its presentation, the idea of embroidering a gyoza-related piece popped back into my mind... so here we go!

### YOU WILL NEED:

- Wool felt with viscose
- Fabric with a little texture and sheen
- Adhesive interlining fabric
- DMC *mouliné* thread
- Clover natural wool roving
- Needles
- Felting needle
- Textile glue
- Cotton or cushion filling
- Clothes pegs

**Stencil on page 118**

To make the gyozas, draw three 10cm (4in) circles onto the fabric and cut them out (1), then place some cotton or cushion filling into the centre of each one.

In the same way as you would with real gyozas, close them from the centre to the sides: make a stitch in the centre, then make a small fold at the front and secure it with another stitch (2, 3).

Continue in this way until you reach the end, but leave one side open to insert some more stuffing into before closing (4, 5, 6).

## Once filled, continue with the same stitches and folds, and close with a knot.

To make the plate, draw a decorative border and print it onto a fabric with a little texture and shine (7). To make it firmer, press a piece of stiff adhesive interlining onto the underside of the fabric.

Paint the edge of the plate with watercolours (8) – I chose bright red – and embroider the patterns on top in a contrasting colour using back stitches – I chose yellow *perlé* thread (9).

I also used a very fine needle and a strand of *mouliné* thread to embroider the detailed tiger logo (10).

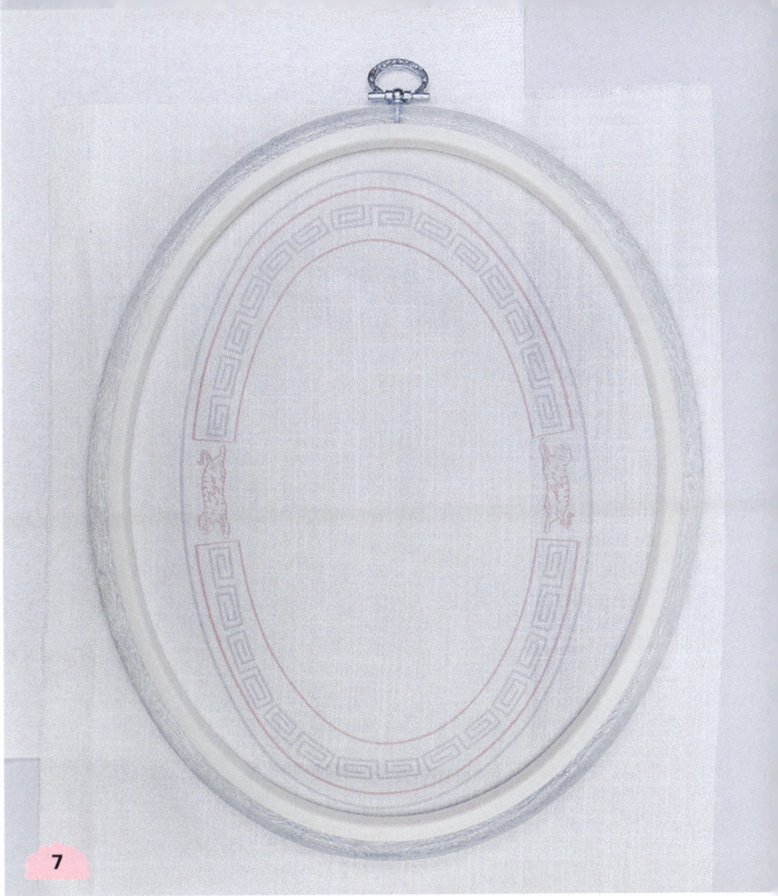

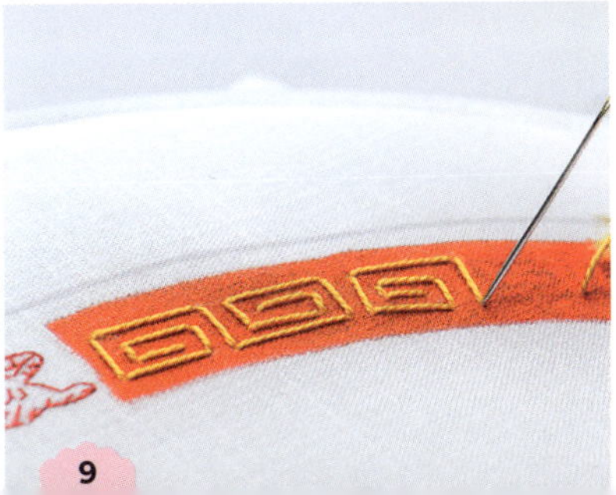

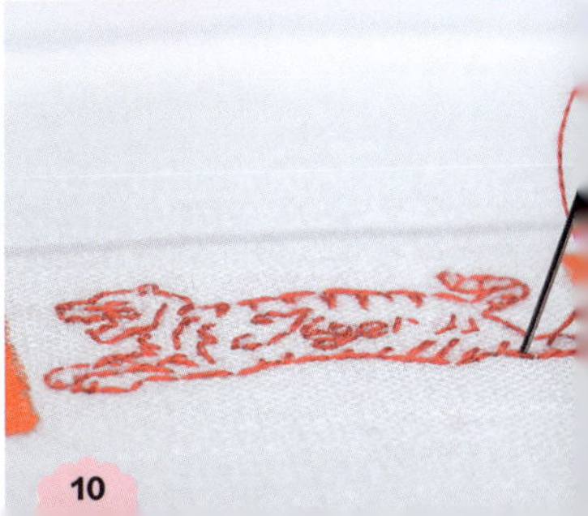

To create the effect of the soy sauce at the base of the plate, add some flat, brown wool roving that won't create too much volume (11). When felting, bear in mind that the more you pass the needle through the wool roving, the flatter the texture will become.

Next, add another layer of adhesive interlining fabric to stiffen the plate (12).

Trim the fabric, leaving a margin of around 2cm (⁴⁄₅in). Make a few small cuts into the excess fabric and attach it to the back of the plate with textile glue. You can use clothes pegs to hold it in place while the glue dries (13). Once dry, glue the piece to the frame (14).

You can leave your gyozas loose on the plate, glue them together or sew them together with a few small stitches, as I did (15).

**For added stability, I would recommend gluing the plate onto an embroidery hoop smaller than the base of the piece.**

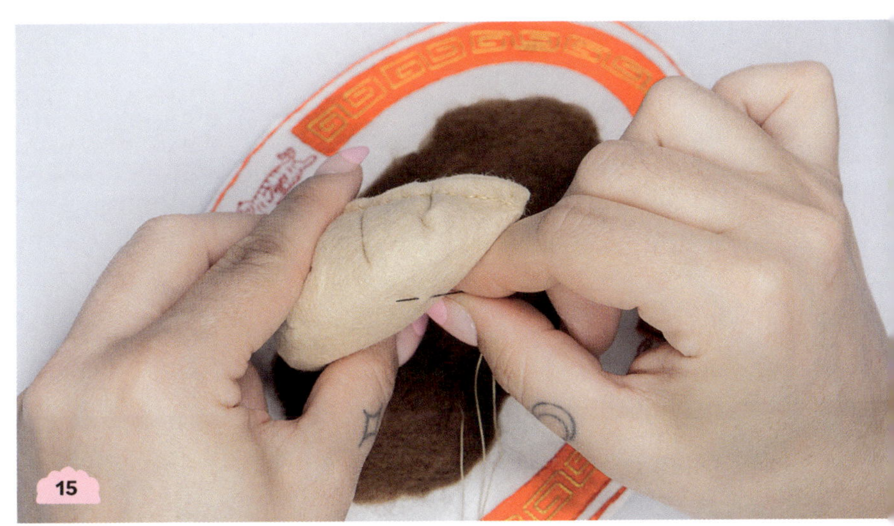

JR
JR東日本
650円
福
福
日本酒
焼きとり
やきとん
TOKU-CHAN
お刺身
ハマグリ
ホタテ

# TOKU CHAN

**When I first walked through the Okachimachi district of Tokyo, I was surprised when I passed an Izakaya restaurant and saw that they had two giant *darumas* at the top of the window.**

*Darumas* are traditional dolls, generally believed to be symbols of good fortune.

There were so many interesting things on the front of the building that I took lots of photos and made a note in my notebook of everything I wanted to embroider.

## YOU WILL NEED:

- Cotton fabric
- DMC *mouliné* thread
- DMC Light Effects thread
- Clover natural wool roving
- Needles
- Felting needle
- Embroidery hoop
- Heat transfer pencil
- Thread wax

**Stencil on page 119**

# I used two small *darumas* that I bought in the Asakusa district to put on the front of the building.

If you have *darumas*, you can cut them in half and make a hole on each side so that you can incorporate them into the piece and create volume (1, 2, 3).

Create the electric cables – found all over Japan – using DMC Light Effects thread, which is very stiff. Wax the thread beforehand to soften it for use. This wax also has the benefit of making the thread, or cables, even stiffer once dry.

Arrange them in long lines from one end to the other, with a small single-strand holding stitch at the bends (4, 5).

2

3

To create the plants at the front of the building, experiment with wool roving (6, 7). When it comes to making vegetation, I always opt for Clover wool because they offer an array of beautiful colours and the finish is incredible.

JR
JR東日本
福
日本酒
焼きとり
やきとん
徳ちゃん
TOKU-CHAN
お刺身
ハマグリ
福
650円

とらふぐ

# FUGU restaurant

## The most fun thing about Japan is seeing the shop fronts and shop signs – they're very flashy!

They aren't usually very large in Tokyo for space reasons, but they are either very funny, because of the drawings on them, or very elegant, made of wood and engraved with *kanji*.

While strolling through the back streets of Shibuya, I came across a restaurant that specialized in *fugu*, a dish made from pufferfish. When I saw the building's display window adorned with a giant fish, I thought 'I have to make this'.

### YOU WILL NEED:

- **Reflective plastic material**
- **Felt**
- **DMC *mouliné* thread**
- **Wool roving**
- **Needles**
- **Embroidery hoop**
- **Textile glue**
- **Heat erasable pen**

**Stencil on page 120**

とらふぐ亭
半額
ご予約は
こちら
03-3462
-7929
当日可能
17:00～22:00
16:00～22:00
半額
半額
半額

**To create the mirrored display, cut a piece of pink and lilac reflective plastic to the desired size and stick it down with textile glue.**

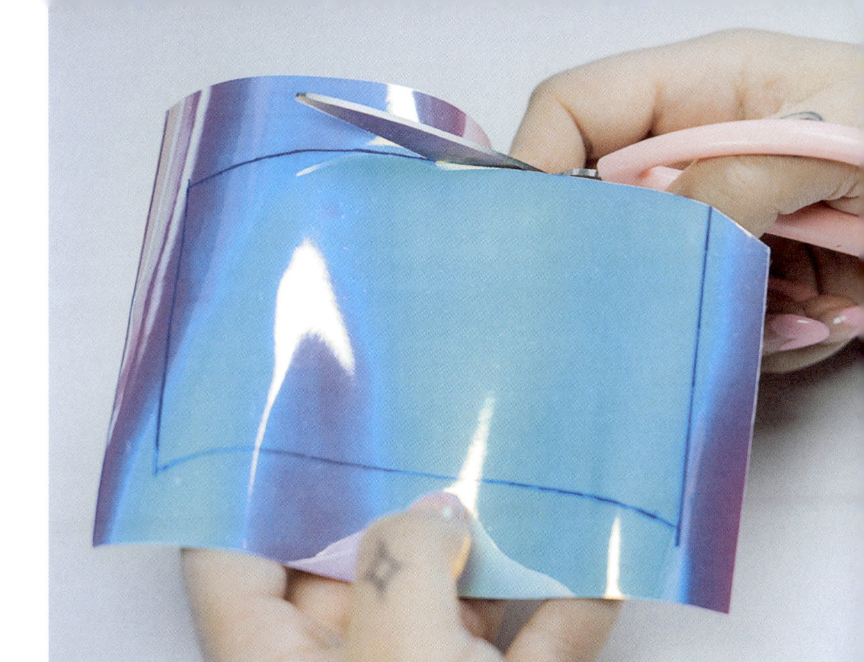

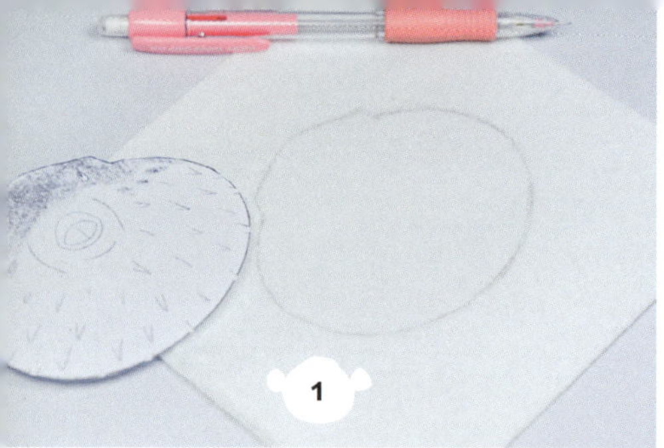

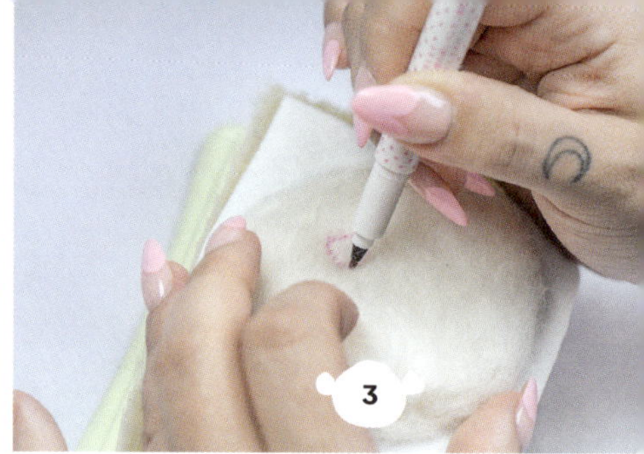


For the *fugu* (the pufferfish), trace the outline onto your felt and add volume with wool roving (1, 2). With the help of a heat erasable pen, mark where each colour and the fish's mouth will go (3).

Embroider the *fugu* with back stitches, using six strands of *mouliné* thread so that the stitches are visible (4, 5).

Prepare the fins using the stumpwork technique.

Cut the felt to the size of the fish (6), then sew the ready-made fins onto the back (7, 8).

Finally, apply textile glue to the back of the fish (9) and position it in the centre of the building's display window (10).

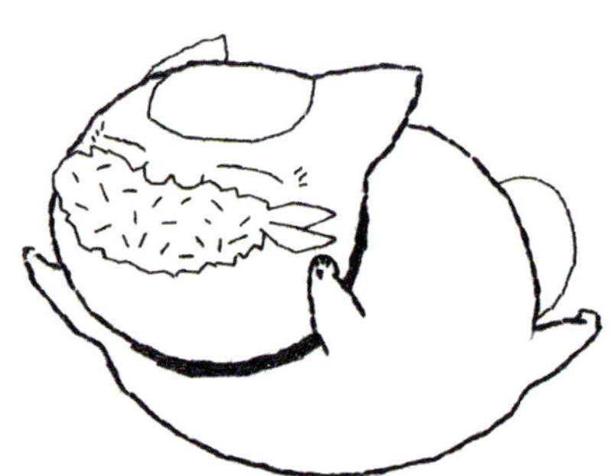

とらふぐ

幸運を
大
商売繁盛

# SAKE barrel

**Sake is one of the most popular Japanese alcoholic beverages. During the Edo period, wooden barrels wrapped in straw and knitted with ropes, called *komodaru*, were specifically designed to transport sake.**

Today, many of these barrels can be found in temples, where they have been left as offerings to the gods. They are also often used to celebrate special occasions, or as part of Shinto rituals.

I have always wanted one of these barrels but couldn't find any for sale, or the ones I could find were enormous, so I decided to make my own *komodaru*.

This project is as special as this book, so I decided to decorate it with a lucky cat for good luck.

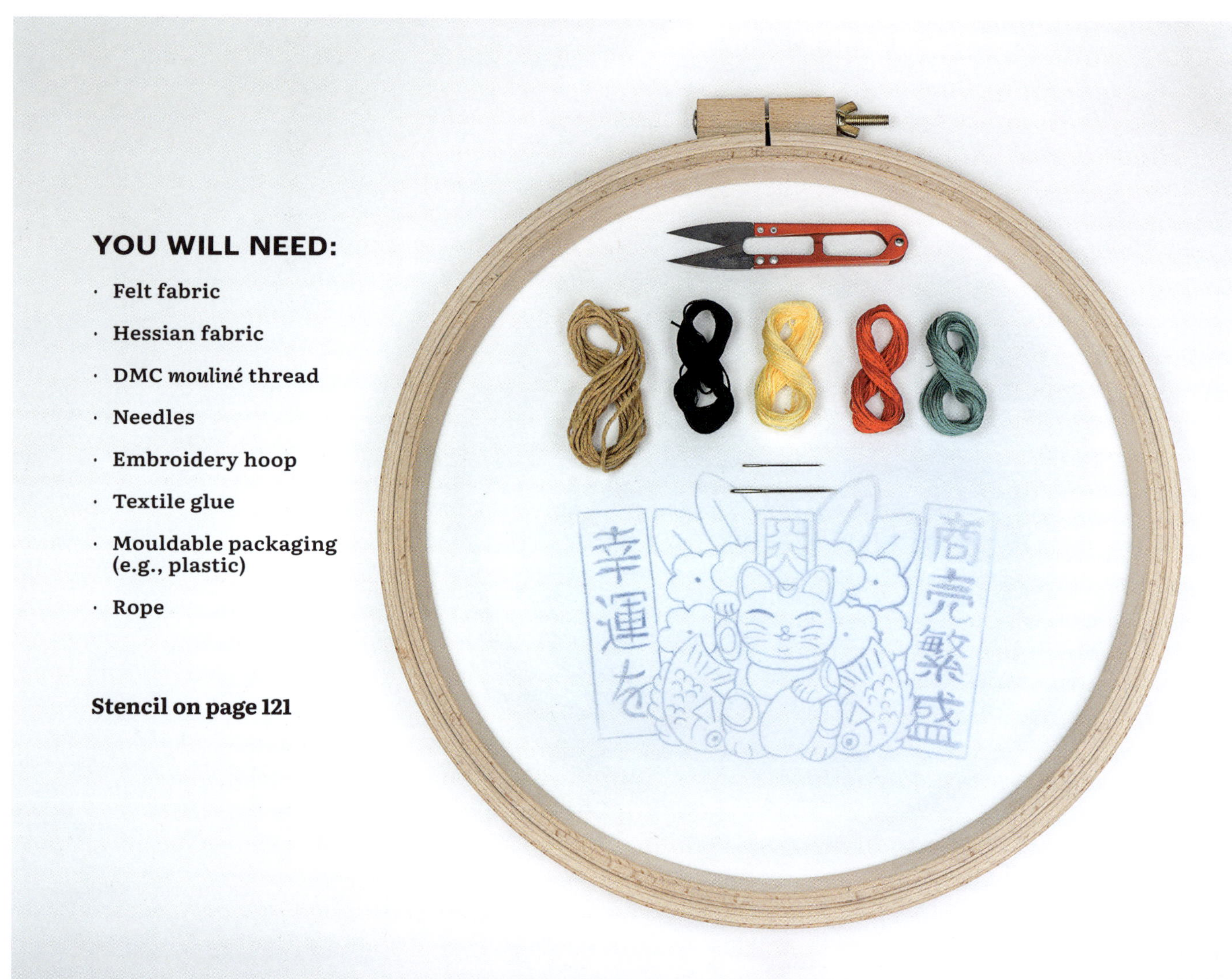


## YOU WILL NEED:

- Felt fabric
- Hessian fabric
- DMC *mouliné* thread
- Needles
- Embroidery hoop
- Textile glue
- Mouldable packaging (e.g., plastic)
- Rope

**Stencil on page 121**

To make a lighter sake barrel, look for an object with a similar barrel-like shape. I eventually found a plastic container that I could reshape into a barrel with some tape (1).

Embroider the design onto your felt.

Wrap the container in the embroidered felt and sew it together at the back, top and bottom (2, 3), as demonstrated in the ‘Final touches’ section on page 26.

To give the barrel a straw-like appearance, add some hessian fabric and secure it with textile glue (4).

Finally, tie the container up with rope, making knots similar to those traditionally used for sake barrels.

1
2
3
4

# AKIHABARA

## If you visit Tokyo, you simply must go to Akihabara, the district of electronics and *otaku* culture. There, you can find camera shops alongside cosplay shops and anime figurine shops... It's paradise!

One thing I make sure never to miss when I'm in Tokyo is visiting Akihabara at night. With its illuminated signs and blaring music, it's one of the most unique places in the city.

---

### YOU WILL NEED:

- Cotton fabric
- DMC *mouliné* thread
- Needles
- Embroidery hoop
- Textile glue
- Heat erasable pen
- Micro LEDs
- Beads

**Stencil on page 122**

When it comes to creating brightly lit nighttime scenes, my favourite gadgets are micro LEDs – they are easy to use and widely available.

**Depending on how far apart you want the LEDs to be placed in the piece, braid them together slightly to ensure they are firmly held in place and secured to the embroidery.**

You can attach them to the fabric with a couple of stitches. You can also pierce the fabric beforehand to make it easier to insert them.

SEGA

SEGA

# TOKYO METRO

## photo transfer

**During one of my trips, we visited a temple on the outskirts of Tokyo. To reach it, we had to travel to the final stop on the train route.**

There was no one left in the carriage and my mind started to imagine *yokais* (supernatural entities and spirits from Japanese folklore) sitting all over the train. Before getting off, I quickly took a photo and sketched an idea in my notebook, which ended up becoming the basis for this project.

Photo transferring is a very simple and versatile technique. You can work on the whole photo or just a part of it, depending on the effect you want.

## YOU WILL NEED:

- Photo transfer paper
- DMC *mouliné* thread
- Printer
- Heat erasable pen

**Stencil on page 123**

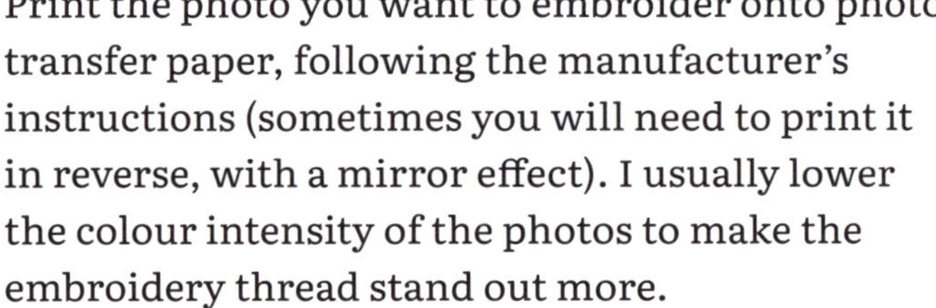

Print the photo you want to embroider onto photo transfer paper, following the manufacturer's instructions (sometimes you will need to print it in reverse, with a mirror effect). I usually lower the colour intensity of the photos to make the embroidery thread stand out more.

This type of paper is usually made for home printing, so you can print the photo as many times as you want.

Iron the printed photo onto your fabric, then wait for it to cool down before sewing onto it.

**Use a heat-erasable pen to sketch your design, then embroider it with your favourite thread.**

Cerâmica - 2.600 W

# KAPPA flowerpot

**Kappabashi is a neighbourhood that specializes in kitchenware and cookery equipment. There are over 150 shops where you can buy anything from bowls and chopsticks to *takoyaki* pans and *kakigori* curtains... you name it, you'll find it here!**

However, the most symbolic thing about this neighbourhood is its mascot: the Japanese mythological creature, the kappa. You'll see depictions of it everywhere: on billboards, statues and amusing decorations on every street corner.

Once, as I approached someone's home, I was greeted by a friendly kappa flowerpot that seemed to welcome me with open arms. I looked for one in the shops, but had no such luck, so I decided to make one myself!

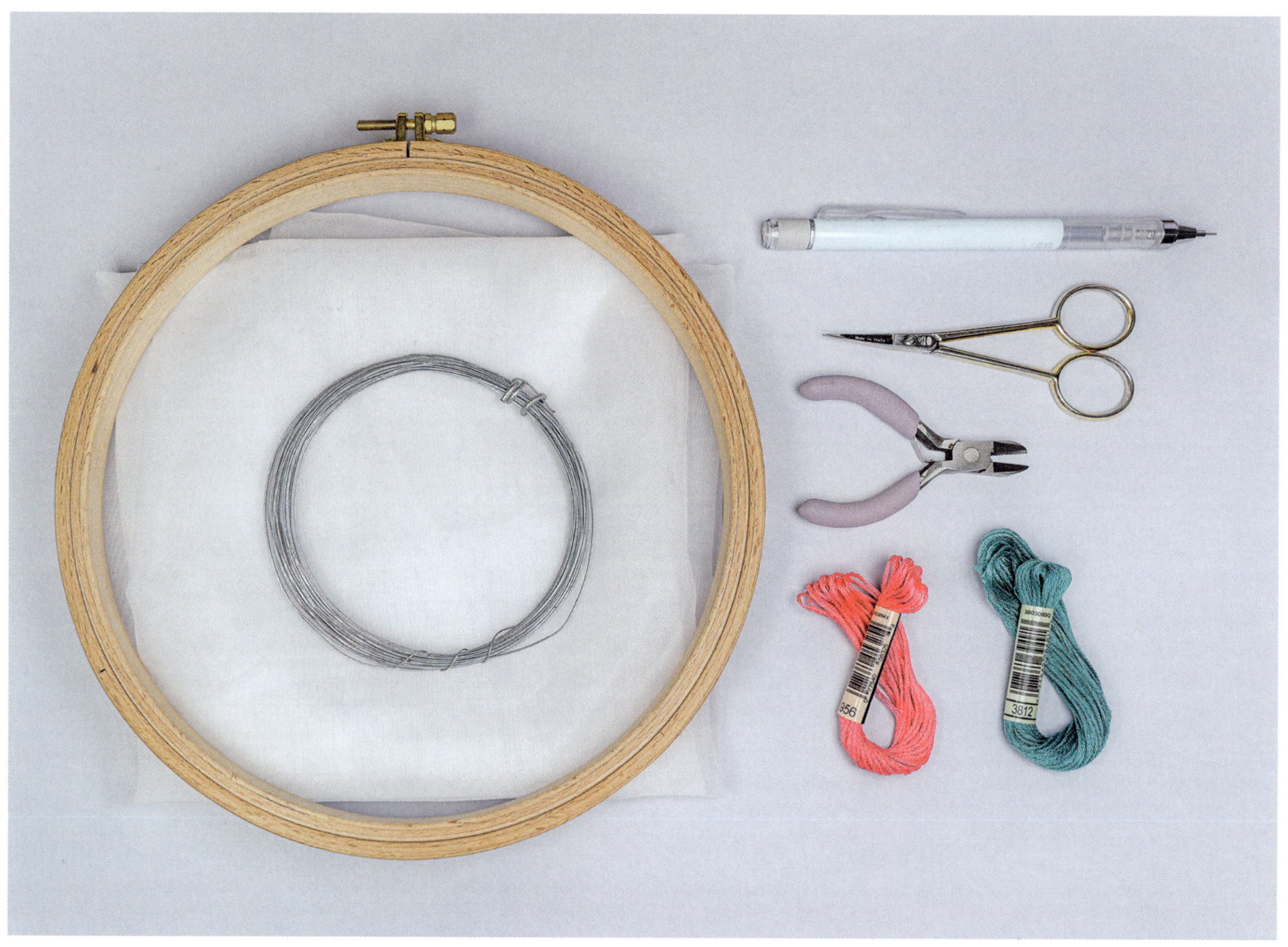


## YOU WILL NEED:

- **Organza fabric**
- **DMC *mouliné* thread**
- **Needles**
- **Embroidery hoop**
- **Wire**

**Stencil on page 124**

Draw the leaves or flowers onto organza fabric (1), then create their shape with a fine wire (2).

Using the same thread that you will use to embroider, use one strand to secure the wire to the fabric with small stitches (3, 4).

Once the wire is secured to the fabric, stitch over it with two or three strands of the same thread (5) until it is completely covered (6).

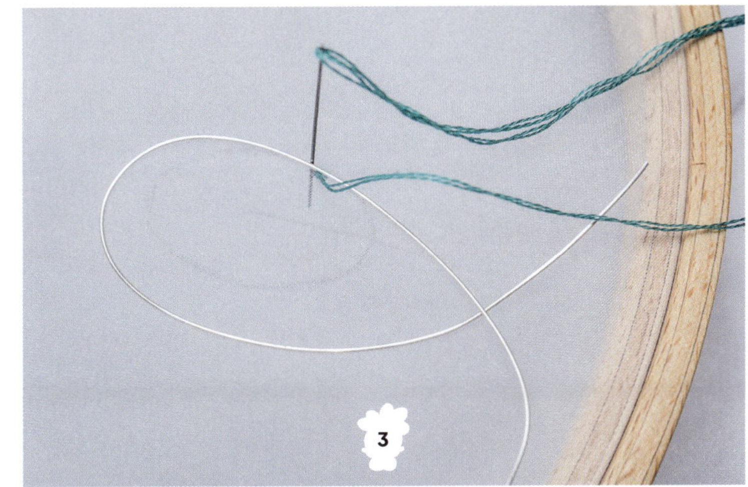
3

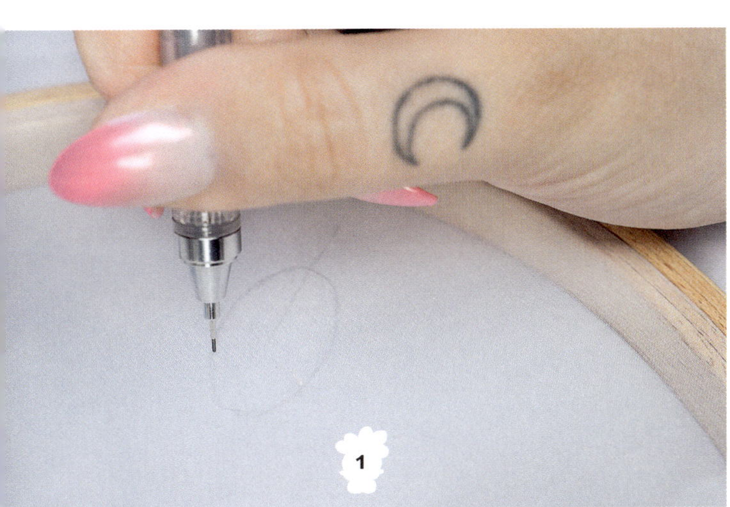
1

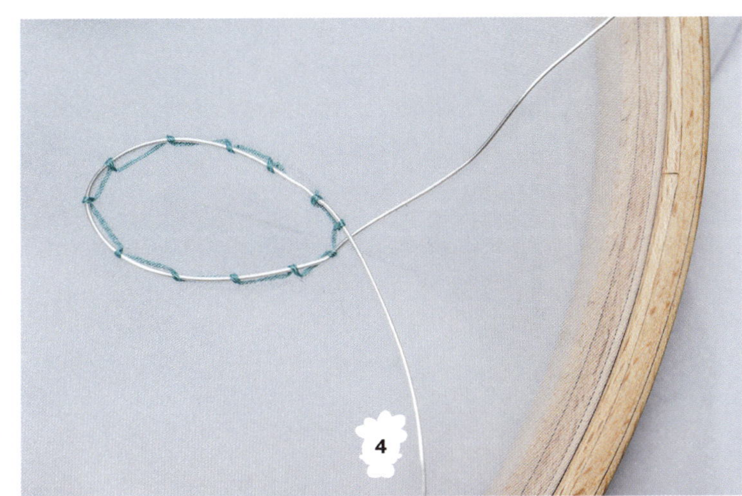
4

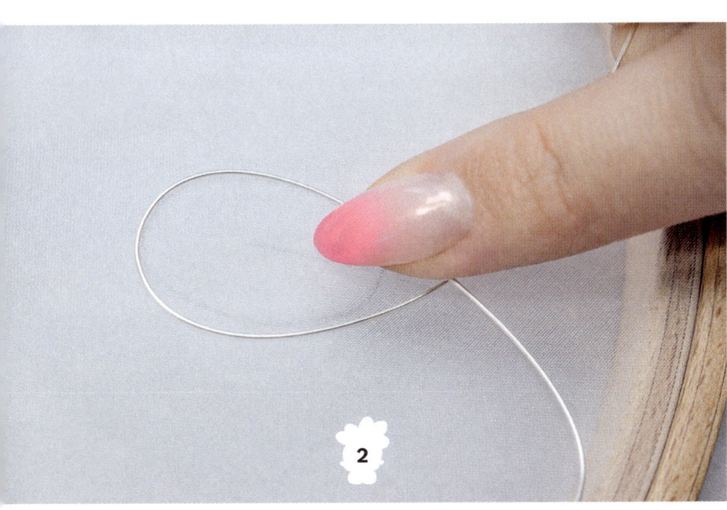
2

5

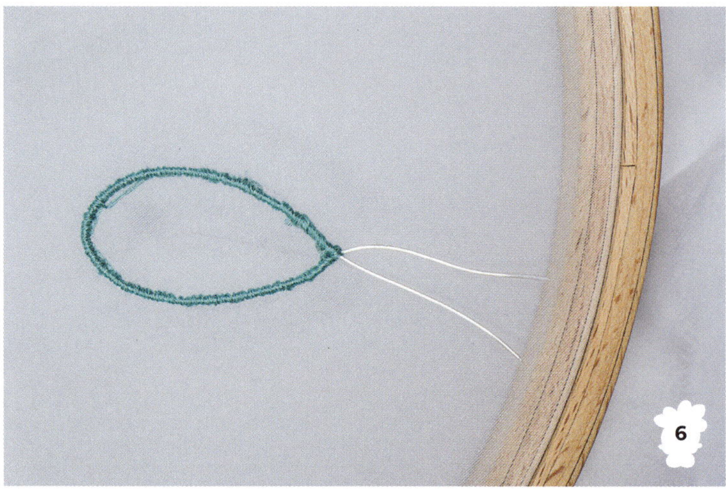

Continue embroidering with satin stitches until you reach the end of the wire. Leave the initial knot in the centre so that you can hide it later, and embroider carefully so that the front and back of each stitch look the same (7). When you run out of thread, tie a very small knot so that it's barely visible.

Repeat the same method for the colour changes: start with a tiny knot and stitch in such a way that both sides end up looking the same (8).

Once you have finished the leaves, trim the organza fabric very close to the wire, taking care not to cut the threads (9).

The stem is simple yet delicate. Start with a very small knot at the base of the leaf, then work your way around the wire. When you have reached the desired length, secure it in place with a finishing stitch (10, 11).

There are a few different ways you can attach the pieces to the embroidery. Some people glue them on, but I prefer to sew them on as this allows you to add new leaves or change them for different designs later. To sew them on, simply make a few stitches between the wire and the fabric (12).

Thanks to the malleability of the wire, once finished, you can give the leaves any shape you like (13, 14).

9

12

10

13

11

14

ALL
100
¥
木子の茶
バードリンク

# VENDING machine

**Would you like a soft drink or a hot coffee? A banana or perhaps a T-shirt? An umbrella?**

**In Japan, you'll find vending machines selling all kinds of things. The products are always good quality and reasonably priced, and the machines are available 24 hours a day.**

What's more, some brands even decorate the outside of the machine in unique ways. One day I came across a vending machine that was painted with Hokusai's *The Great Wave off Kanagawa*, from the Edo period. It's one of my favourite prints so, naturally, I wanted to recreate it.

## YOU WILL NEED:

- Cotton fabric
- Water-soluble fabric
- Leftover metallic fabric
- White felt
- DMC *mouliné* thread
- Needles
- Embroidery hoop
- Cardboard
- Textile glue
- Sequins
- Micro LEDs
- Rectangular canvas

**Stencil on page 125**

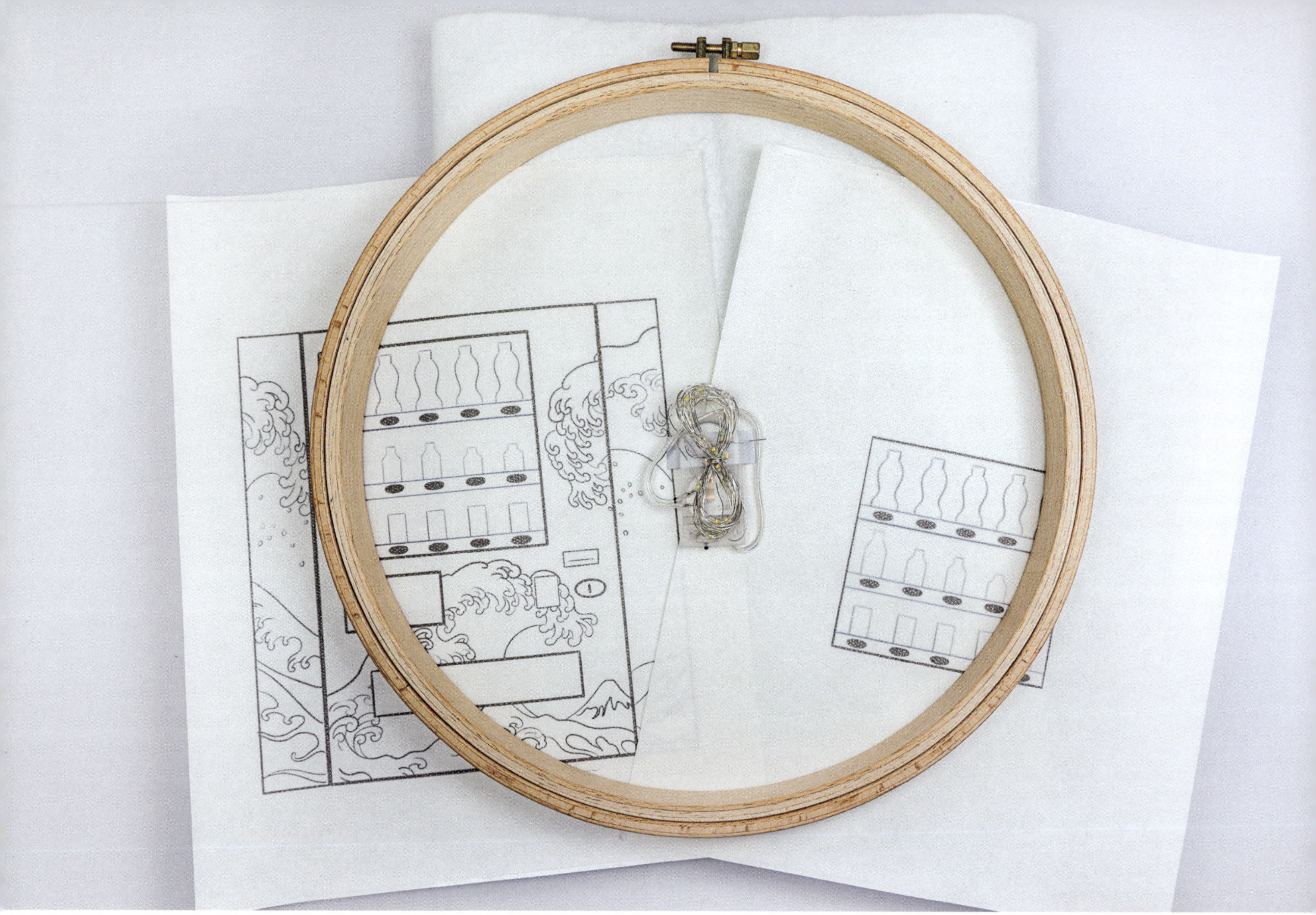

**This design is made up of two parts: a base featuring embroidered drinks and a three-dimensional machine.**

Prepare the base on a cotton canvas by painting the background with watercolour and embroidering the drinks (1).

Print the wave design onto water-soluble fabric and then embroider it onto white felt, so that the characteristic blue tone of the original illustration is visible (2, 3).

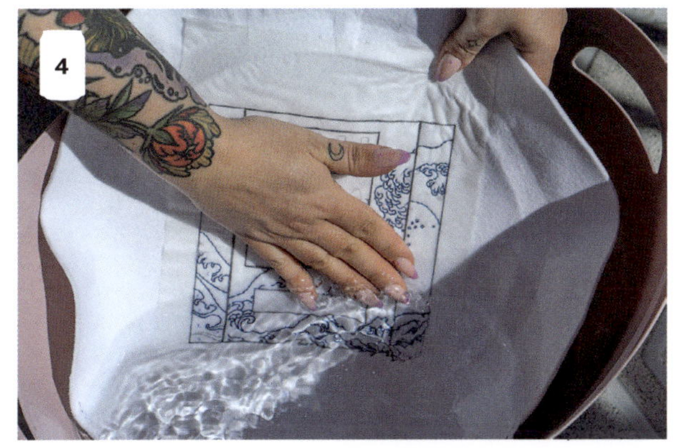


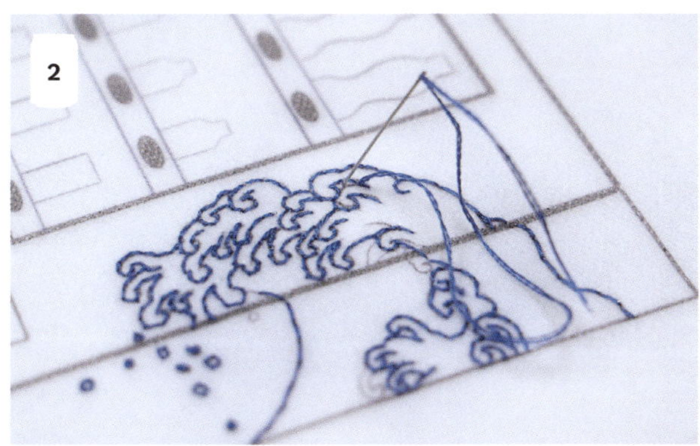

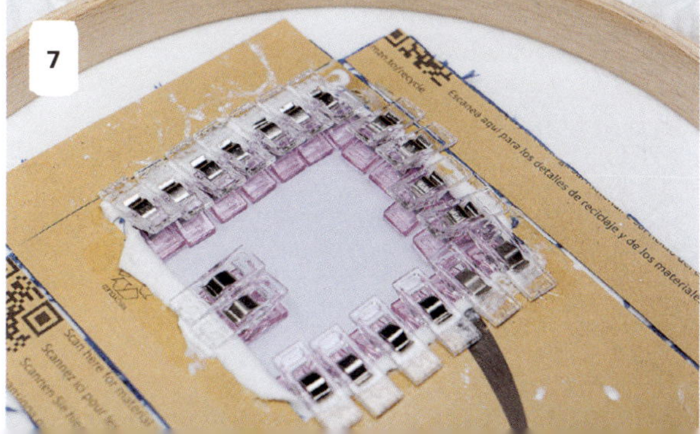

Once you have finished the piece, dampen and rub the water-soluble fabric so that it gradually disappears (4).

To make your machine more rigid, attach some pieces of cardboard to the felt using textile glue (5, 6, 7).

If you want to add a quirky detail, cut a piece of metallic fabric (it can be the same fabric we used for the *fugu* fish on page 68), and attach it to the slot where the drinks come out. Then, embroider some sequins onto the fabric to look like the feet of the vending machine (8, 9).

Sew the sides of the tabs together to create the machine (10).

For the filling, stack several layers of felt together (11, 12). Before gluing on the final layer, embroider an LED strip onto the top using small stitches (13, 14).

11

12

13

14

**To finish the piece and show it off, line a rectangular canvas with fabric and cut a small hole in the centre through which to thread the battery pack. This will hide the battery pack and make it easier to handle.**

# KOI fish

**The first time I saw a koi pond, there were so many fish that it was impossible to count them, and they were huge!**

They have a special glow that captivates you as you watch them move from side to side. It's one of my fondest memories from my first trip to Japan years ago, so I wanted to bring it back to life.

## YOU WILL NEED:

- Felt fabric
- Tulle fabric
- Blue cotton fabric
- DMC *mouliné* thread
- DMC *étoile* thread
- DMC tapestry wool (also known as Colbert wool)
- Clover natural wool roving
- Needles
- Felting needle
- Small stones
- Two embroidery hoops of the same size
- White Posca marker pen
- Textile glue

**Stencil on page 126**

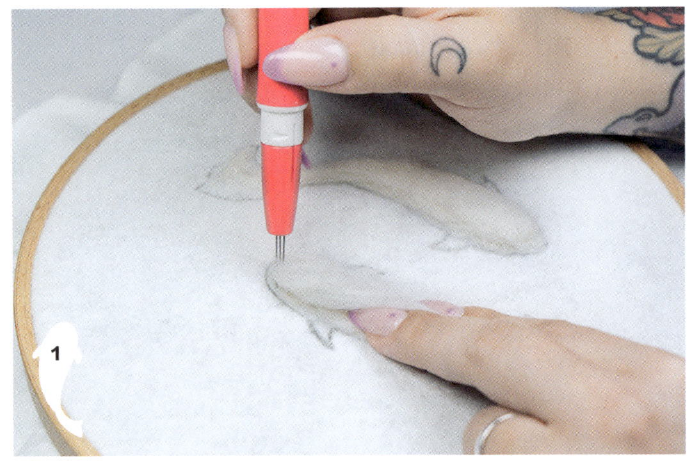

**This piece has two levels, which helps to give the impression that the fish are swimming in the water.**

Draw the fish onto a piece of felt and add volume to them using the felting technique (1).

Embroider the fish with *étoile* thread, which is incredibly shiny and easy to handle, and cut them out (2, 3).

Fix the tulle fabric to your hoop and attach the fish to it with a strand of thread (4, 5).

Use the Colbert wool to embroider details such as water lily leaves or water plants: make loops, cut the ends and tousle the thread a little with a comb (6, 7, 8, 9).

Draw and then paint the pond water onto the blue cotton fabric using the Posca marker pen, then place it onto another hoop of the same size (10).

Join the two frames together with wood or plastic glue, depending on the material (11).

With glue, attach some small stones around the edge of the hoop (12, 13).

Then, stitch the hoops together with green thread to prevent them from separating and to enhance the pond effect (14).

12

13

14

TAKESHITA ST.
WEGO
WEGO
MOCHA CAT
CAT CAFE
1F.
¥300
吉野家
YOSHINOYA
PUCK

## Both Takeshita Street and the Harajuku district are undoubtedly must-sees; I can easily spend a whole day there!

Takeshita Street is a beautiful and colourful street. As soon as you leave Harajuku Station, you come across an archway of balloons inviting you to enter.

The archway is decorated according to the season: at Christmas, there are trees and presents; in spring, there are pink *sakura* flowers... It's always colourful and cheerful!

Takeshita is all about the colour pink and pastel shades. You can find everything here, from cosmetic products, contact lenses, spiral-shaped crisps, *kawaii* and *lolita* clothes, to heart-shaped cotton candy, ice cream shaped like a cat's face and crêpes with such incredible decorations that you'll feel guilty eating them.

# TAKESHITA Street

## YOU WILL NEED:

- Cotton fabric
- DMC *mouliné* thread
- Clover natural wool roving
- Needles
- Felting needle
- Embroidery hoop
- Heat erasable pen
- Assorted beads

**Stencil on page 127**

The highlight of this project is the famous entrance archway, full of colour and balloons.

I recreated the balloons in the embroidery with beads, trying to make them as similar in shape as possible.

Remember to place the beads carefully, only doing so once you have finished the embroidered parts with thread so that they don't damage the piece.

I made the 'Takeshita St.' sign using heart-shaped beads, which I painted with a matte mint spray paint, before adding the letters by hand with a paintbrush.

TAKESHITA
WEGO
¥300
CAT CAFE
MOGCHA CAT
WEGO
1F.

# MORE IDEAS AND PROJECTS

Nurge
XT STATION
ELEVEN
mister
Donut
Milky
NEXT STATIO
TOKYO
MAP

# ARI GATO!

This book would not have been possible without the resolve of my husband, Guindero, who has supported me through my craziness for so many years, without the Panta Rhei family, who have helped me time and time again to keep going since the day we met, and without Mónica from Núvol de Fils, who saw my art and encouraged me along this path.

I would also like to thank key brands such as Clover Japan, DMC España and Nurge, who all believed in me and my work.

My thanks also go out to the students of my workshops and to my followers, who show me love and support at every event.

Also to Aina and Editorial GG for giving me this fabulous opportunity.

And last, but not least, to Alba for your art, your photographs and, above all, for the wonderful months spent working side by side in our craziness.

THANK YOU & ARIGATOOO! :)

# TAIYAKI PINCUSHION

Page 30

**Back stitch**
① DMC *coton perlé* no. 5 780
(All lines)

# RAMEN BROOCH

Page 36

**Satin stitch**

① DMC *mouliné* 743
② DMC *mouliné Blanc*
③ DMC *mouliné* 3859
④ DMC *mouliné* 677

**Back stitch**

❶ DMC *mouliné* 310
(All bordering lines)
❷ DMC *mouliné* 501
❸ DMC *mouliné* 3801
❹ DMC *mouliné Blanc*
❺ DMC *mouliné* 956
❻ DMC *mouliné* 842

**French knot**

❶ 907
❷ DMC *coton perlé* 8972

# SHINJUKU 3D CAT

Page 42

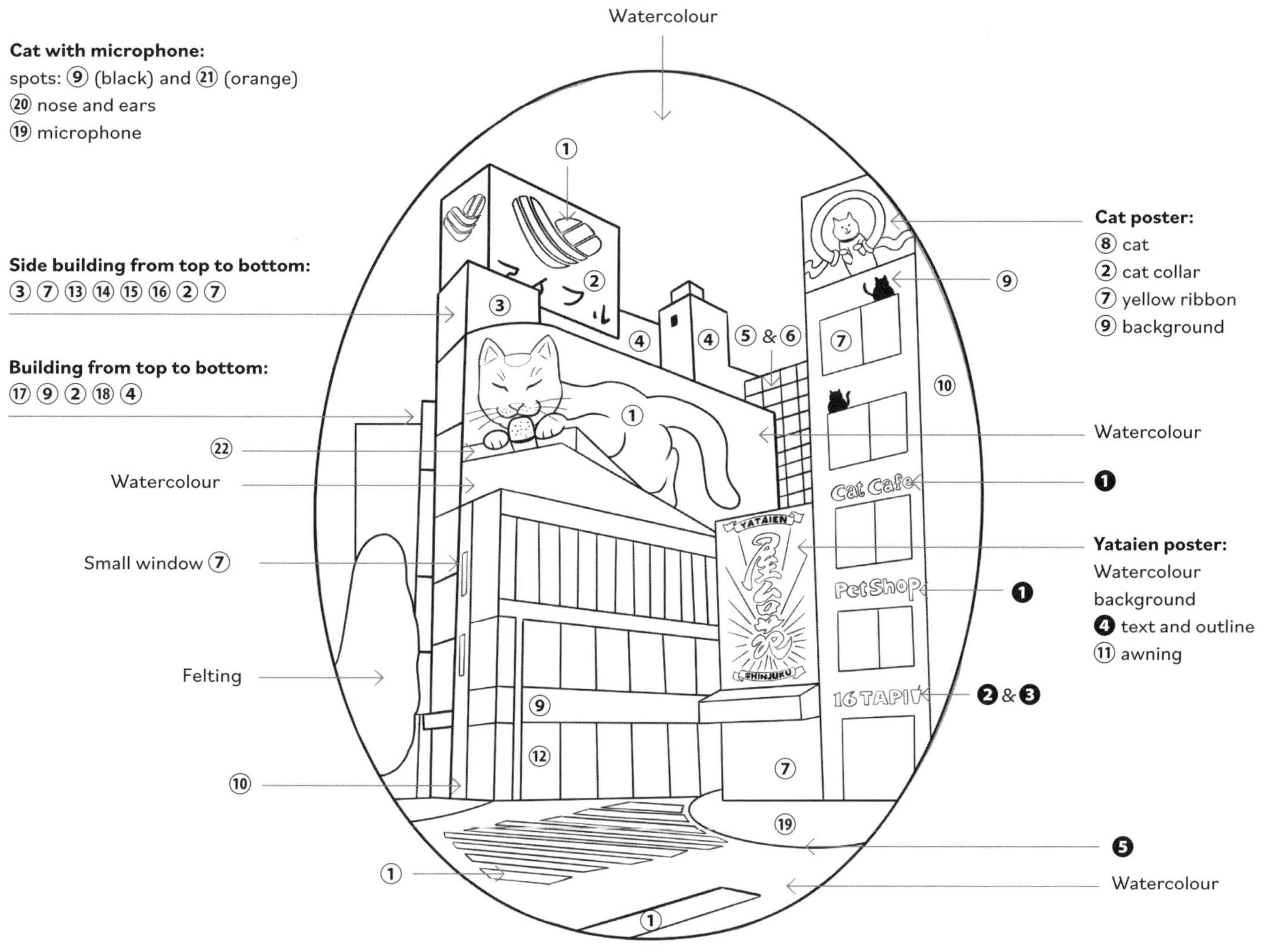


**Satin stitch**
① DMC *mouliné Blanc*
② DMC *mouliné* 666
③ DMC *mouliné* 3760
④ DMC *mouliné* 169
⑤ DMC *mouliné* 726
⑥ DMC *mouliné* 28
⑦ DMC *mouliné* 744
⑧ DMC *mouliné* 842
⑨ DMC *mouliné* 310
⑩ DMC *mouliné* 318
⑪ DMC *mouliné* 3801
⑫ DMC *mouliné* 745
⑬ DMC *mouliné* 892
⑭ DMC *mouliné* 775
⑮ DMC *mouliné* 211
⑯ DMC *mouliné* 955
⑰ DMC *mouliné* 996
⑱ DMC *mouliné* 155
⑲ DMC *mouliné* 02
⑳ DMC *mouliné* 3689
㉑ DMC *mouliné* 722
㉒ DMC *mouliné* 644

**Back stitch**
❶ DMC *mouliné Blanc*
❷ DMC *mouliné* 966
❸ DMC *mouliné* 824
❹ DMC *mouliné* 744
❺ DMC *mouliné* 726
❻ DMC *mouliné* 310
(All black lines)

**For the felting**
Clover natural wool roving 7922

# SWEETS HOTEL

Page 48

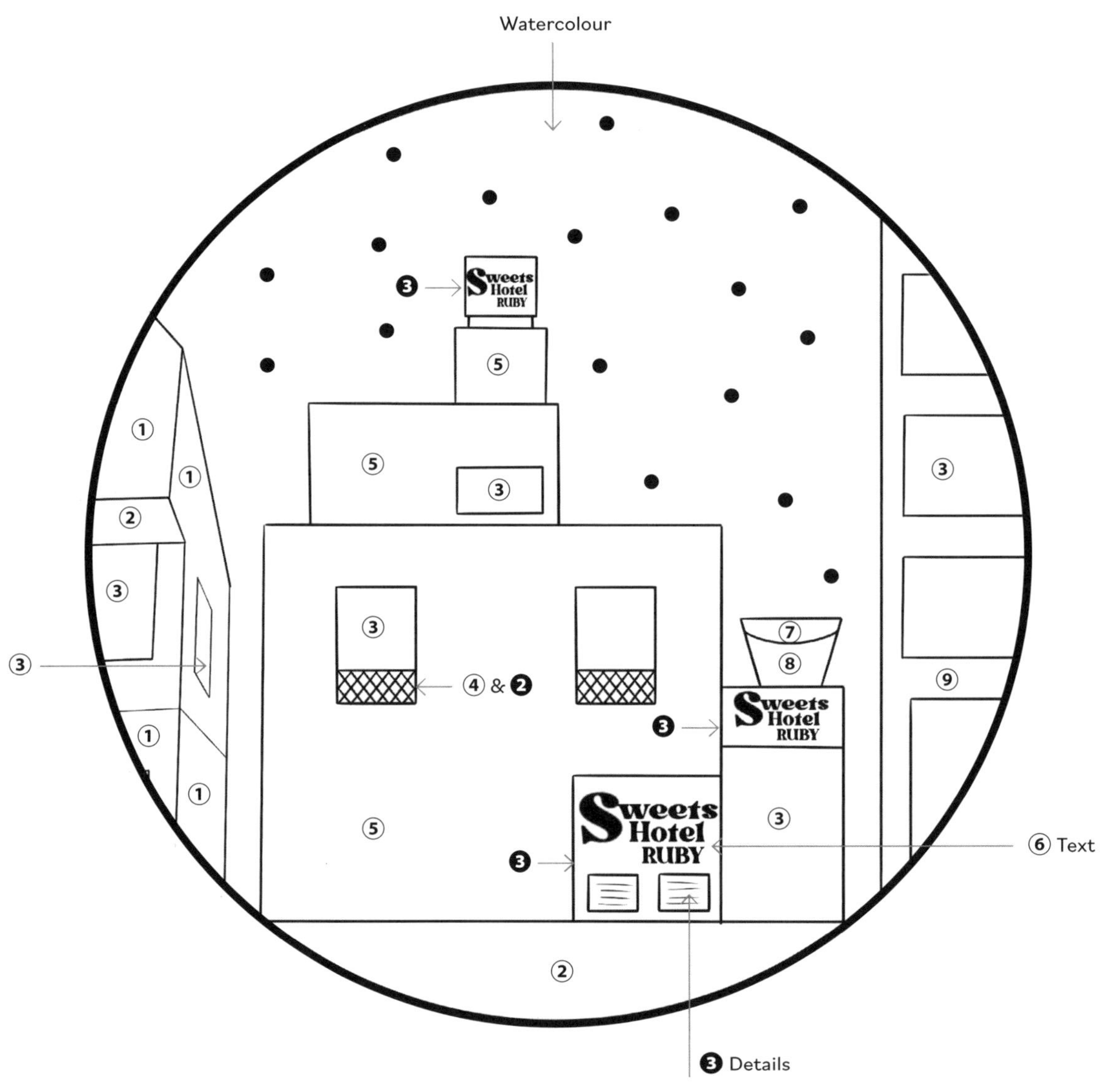


**Satin stitch**

① DMC *mouliné* 415
② DMC *mouliné* 414
③ DMC *mouliné* 745
④ DMC *mouliné* 602
⑤ DMC *mouliné* 894
⑥ DMC *mouliné* 413
⑦ DMC *mouliné* 666
⑧ DMC *mouliné Blanc*
⑨ DMC *mouliné* 168

**Back stitch**

❶ DMC *mouliné* 310
(All black lines)
❷ DMC *mouliné* 414
❸ DMC *mouliné* 208

# MANHOLE COVERS

Page 52

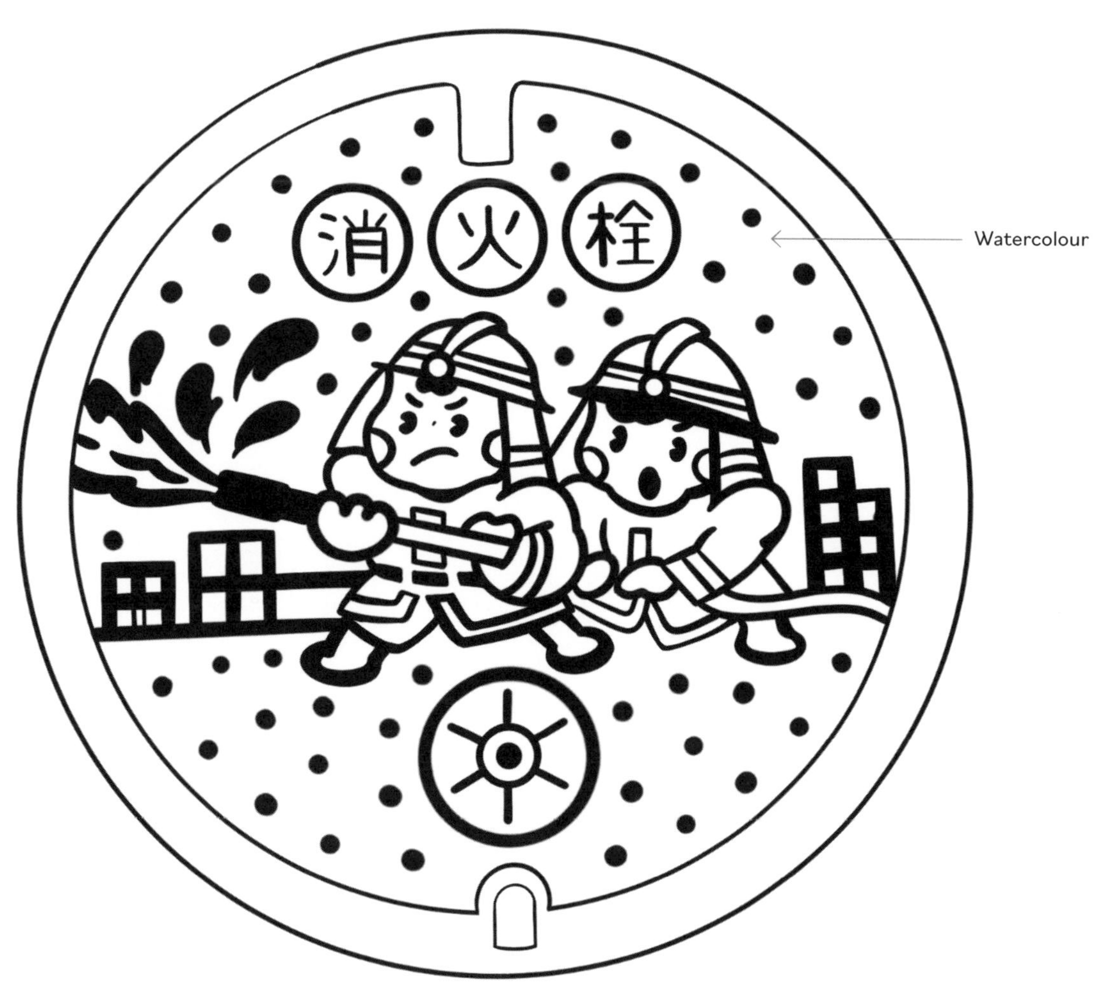


**Back stitch**
❶ DMC *mouliné* 310
(All black lines and details)

# GYOZA TIGER

Page 56

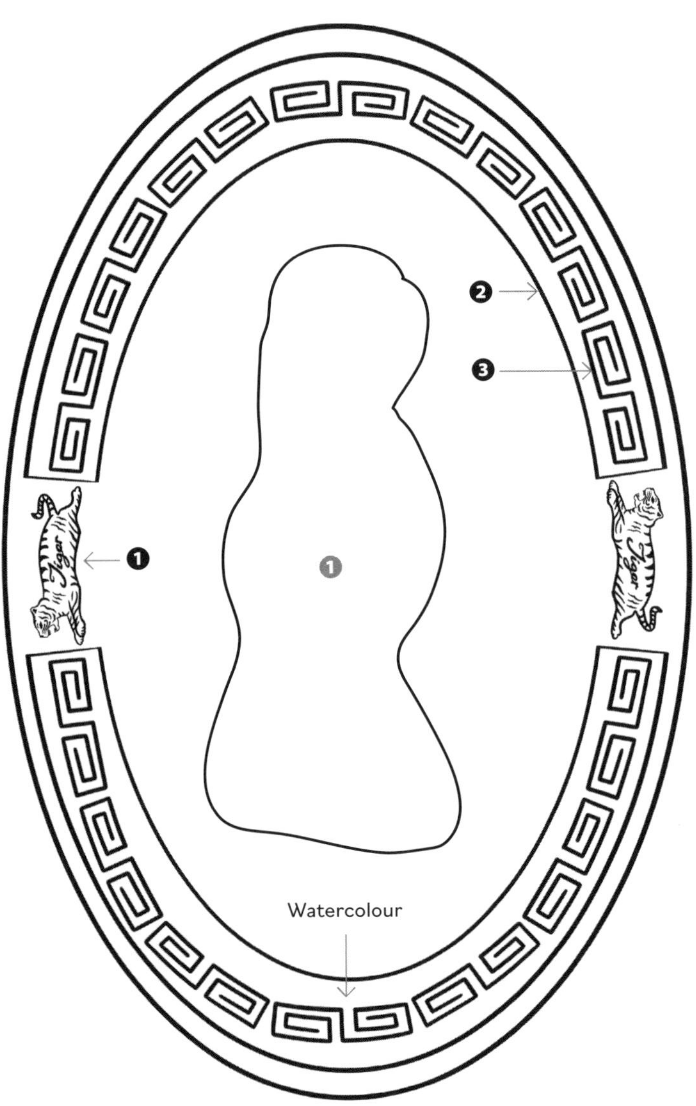


**Back stitch**

❶ DMC *mouliné* 666 (1 strand)
❷ DMC *mouliné* 666 (6 strands)
❸ DMC *coton perlé* no. 8 972

**For the felting**

❶ Clover natural wool roving 7935

# TOKU-CHAN

Page 62

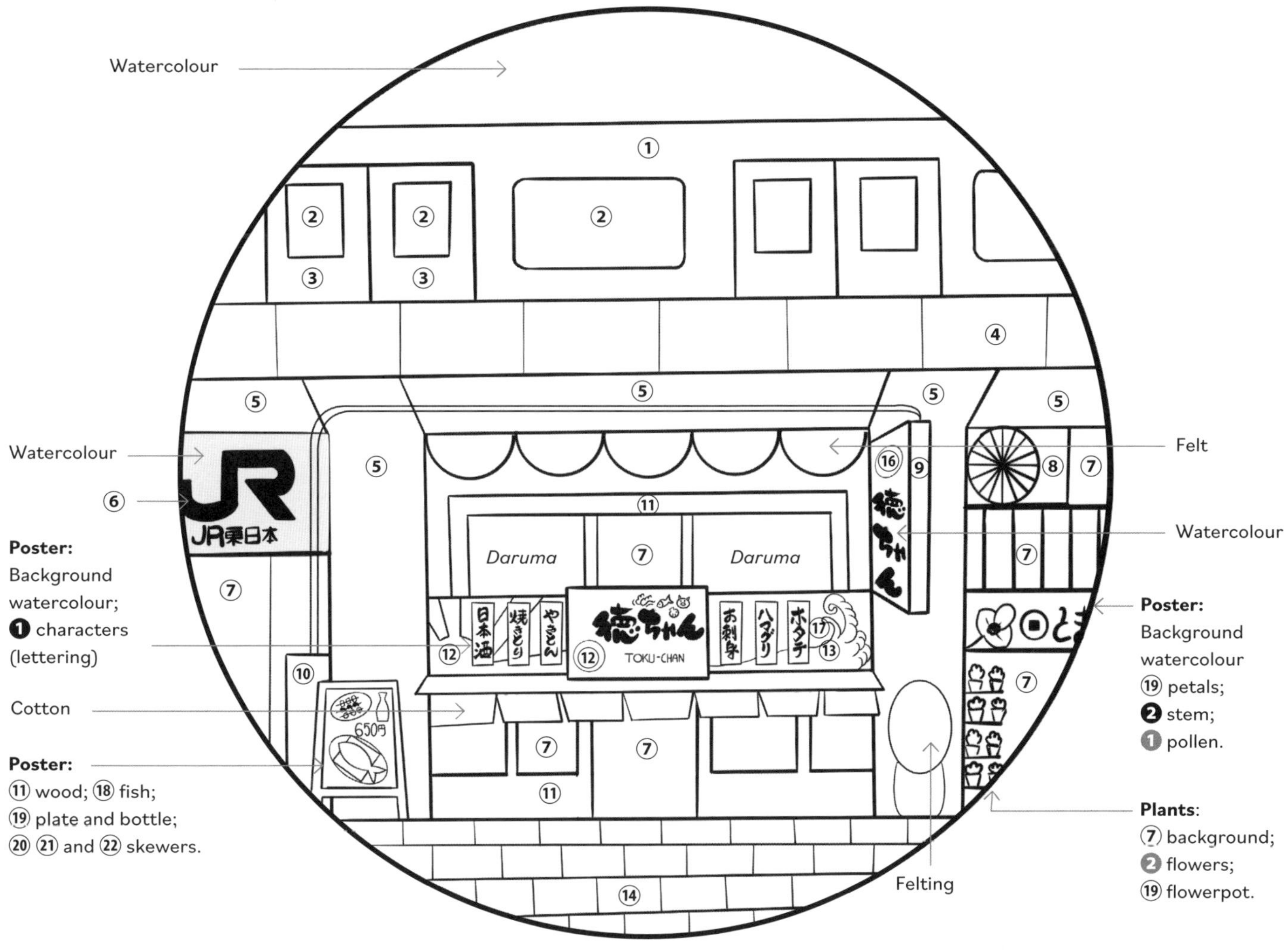


**Satin stitch**

① DMC *mouliné* 964
② DMC *mouliné* 745
③ DMC *mouliné* 992
④ DMC *mouliné* 318
⑤ DMC *mouliné* 414
⑥ DMC *mouliné* 913
⑦ DMC *mouliné* 744
⑧ DMC *mouliné* 02
⑨ DMC *mouliné* 3799
⑩ DMC *mouliné* 413
⑪ DMC *mouliné* 3864
⑫ DMC *mouliné* 3801
⑬ DMC *mouliné* 3760
⑭ DMC *mouliné* 3042
⑮ DMC *mouliné* 3859
⑯ DMC *mouliné* 666
⑰ DMC *mouliné* 950
⑱ DMC *mouliné* 3747
⑲ DMC *mouliné Blanc*
⑳ DMC *mouliné* 300
㉑ DMC *mouliné* 906
㉒ DMC *mouliné* 605

**Back stitch**

❶ DMC *mouliné* 310
(All black lines)
❷ DMC *mouliné* 964

**French knot**

➊ DMC *mouliné* 3801
➋ DMC *mouliné* 891

**For the cables**

DMC Light Effects E310

**For the felting**

Clover natural wool roving 7922

# FUGU RESTAURANT

Page 68

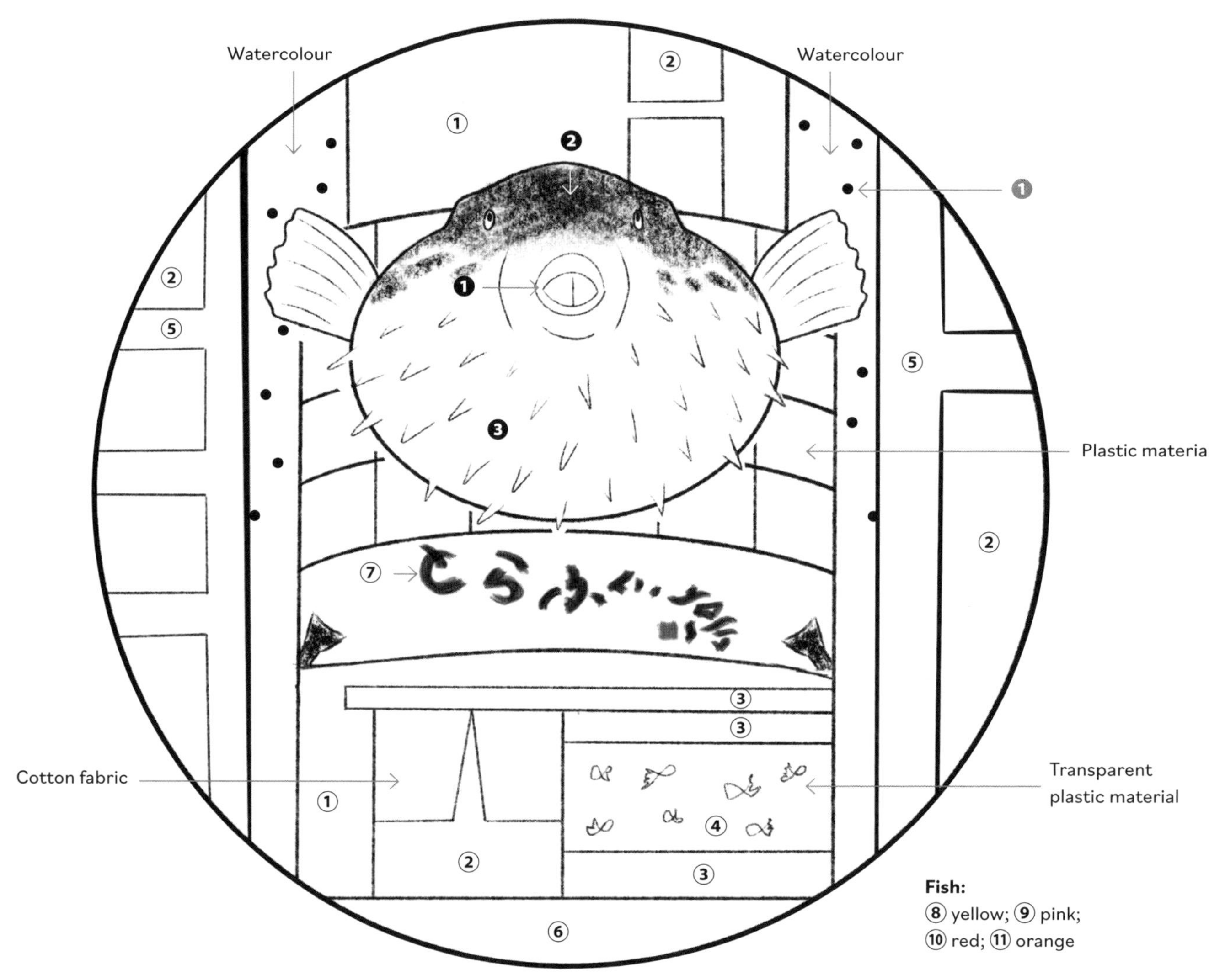


**Satin stitch**

① DMC *mouliné* 317
② DMC *mouliné* 744
③ DMC *mouliné* 415
④ DMC *mouliné* 813
⑤ DMC *mouliné* 415
⑥ DMC *mouliné* 169
⑦ DMC *mouliné* 3799
⑧ DMC *mouliné* 444
⑨ DMC *mouliné* 605
⑩ DMC *mouliné* 817
⑪ DMC *mouliné* 970

**Back stitch**

❶ DMC *mouliné* 834
❷ DMC *mouliné* 844
❸ DMC *mouliné* 3866
❹ DMC *mouliné* 310
(All black lines)

**French knot**

❶ DMC *mouliné* 3822

**For the felting**

Clover natural wool roving 7920

# SAKE BARREL

Page 74

**Satin stitch**

① DMC *mouliné* 666

**Back stitch**

❶ DMC *mouliné* 321
❷ DMC *mouliné* 913
❸ DMC *mouliné* 3713
❹ DMC *mouliné* 3822
❺ DMC *mouliné* 310
❻ DMC *mouliné* 666
❼ DMC *mouliné Blanc*
❽ DMC *mouliné* 310
(All black lines)

# AKIHABARA

Page 78

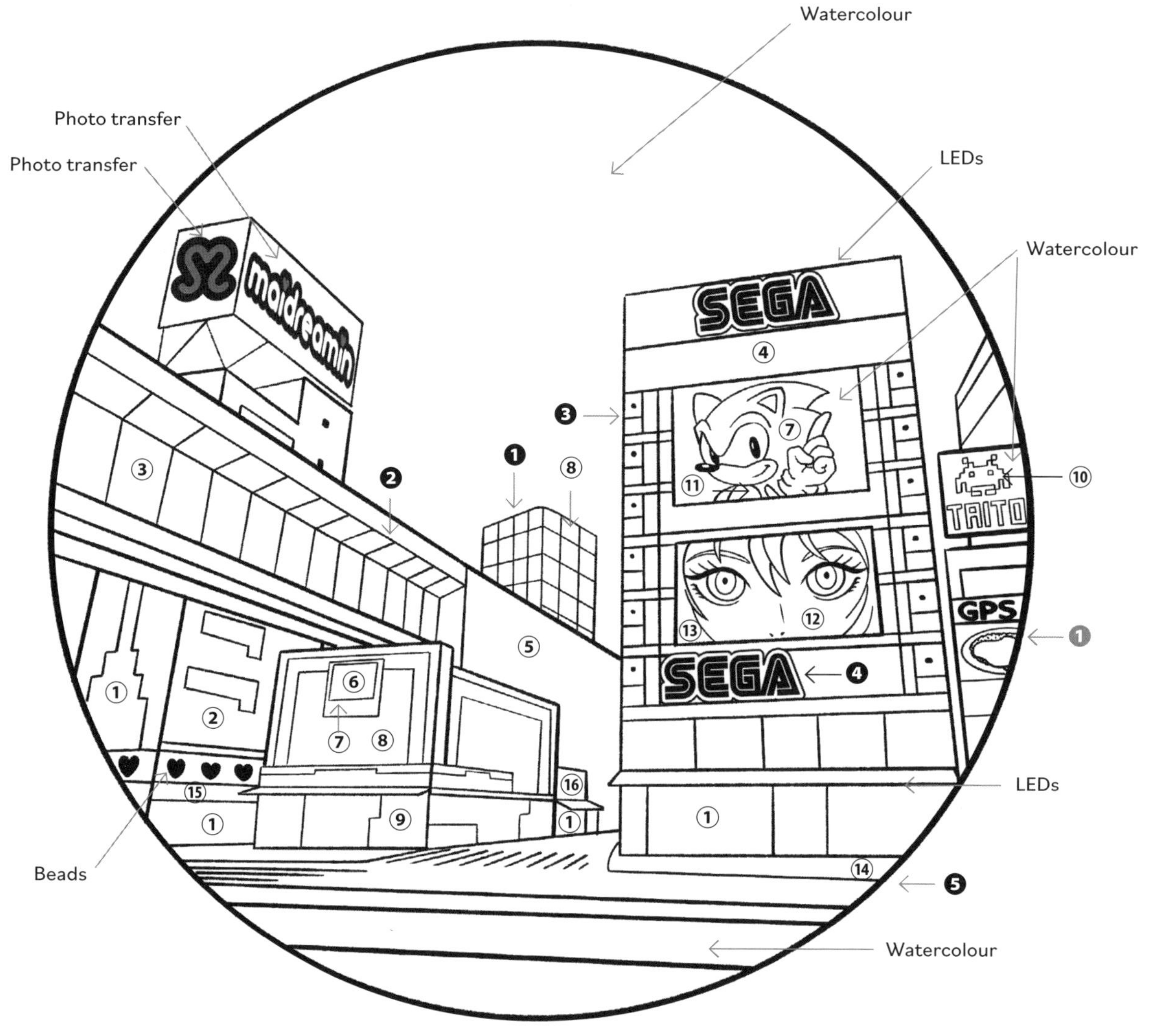


**Satin stitch**

① DMC *mouliné* 745
② DMC *mouliné* 318
③ DMC *mouliné* 992
④ DMC *mouliné* 321
⑤ DMC *mouliné* 341
⑥ DMC *mouliné* 743
⑦ DMC *mouliné* 517
⑧ DMC *mouliné* 3743
⑨ DMC *mouliné* 926
⑩ DMC *mouliné Blanc*
⑪ DMC *mouliné* 950
⑫ DMC *mouliné* 819
⑬ DMC *mouliné* 3846
⑭ DMC *mouliné* 02
⑮ DMC *mouliné* 605
⑯ DMC *mouliné* 3839

**Back stitch**

❶ DMC *mouliné* 154
❷ DMC *mouliné* 310
(All black lines)
❸ DMC *mouliné Blanc*
❹ DMC *mouliné* 995
❺ DMC *mouliné* 743

**French knot**

❶ DMC *mouliné Blanc*

# TOKYO METRO PHOTO TRANSFER

Page 82

**Satin stitch**
① DMC *mouliné* 24
② DMC *étoile* C444
③ DMC *étoile* C938
④ DMC *étoile* C433
⑤ DMC *mouliné* 444

⑥ DMC *mouliné Blanc*
⑦ DMC *étoile* C666
⑧ DMC *mouliné* 310
⑨ DMC *mouliné* 02
⑩ DMC *mouliné* 819

⑪ DMC *étoile* 3799
⑫ DMC *étoile* C471
⑬ DMC *étoile* C725
⑭ DMC *étoile* C310
⑮ DMC *mouliné* 3713

**Back stitch**
❶ DMC *mouliné* 310
(All black lines)
❷ DMC *mouliné* 819

# KAPPA FLOWERPOT

Page 86

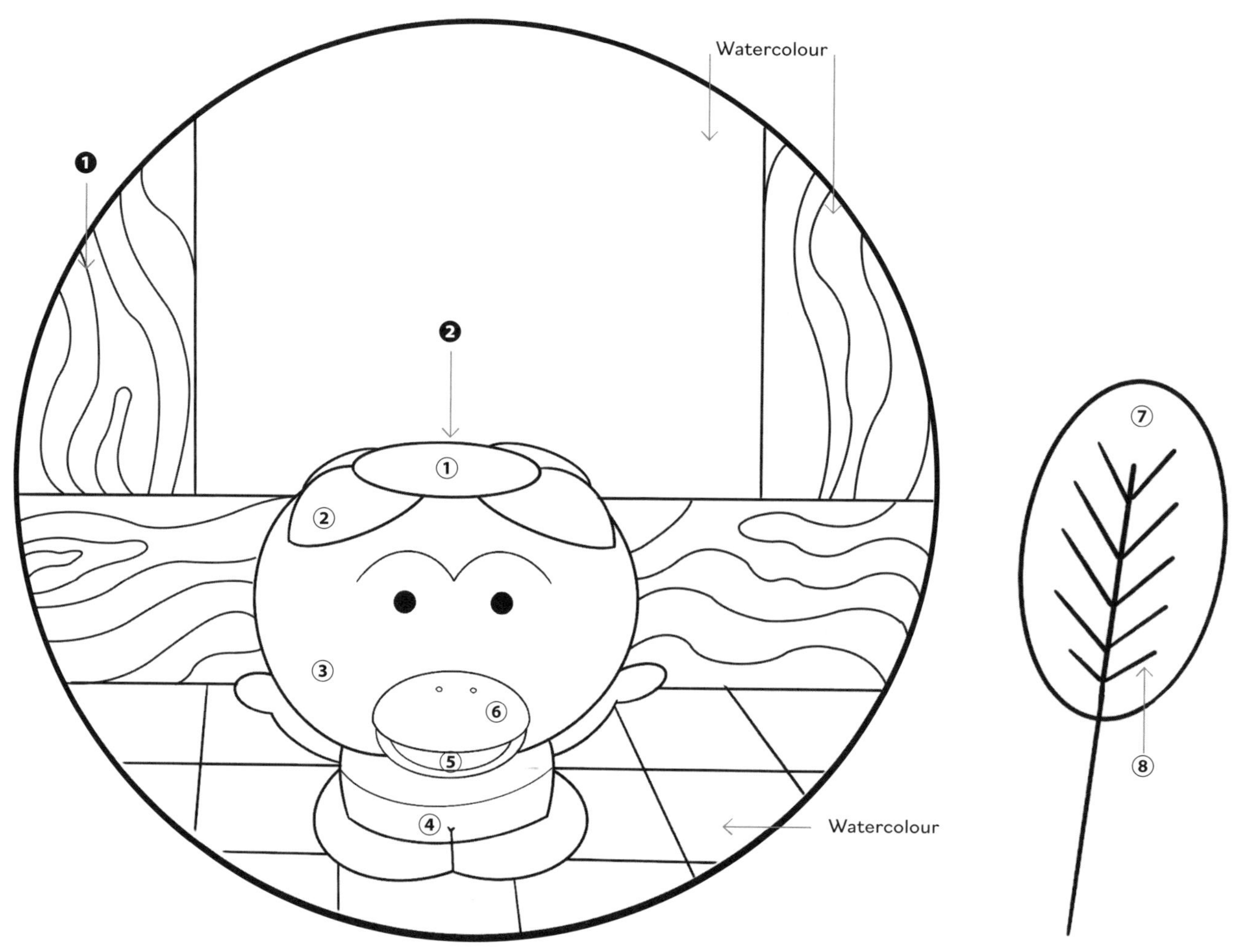


**Satin stitch**

① DMC *mouliné* 320
② DMC *mouliné* 954
③ DMC *mouliné* 3078
④ DMC *mouliné* 3766
⑤ DMC *mouliné* 957
⑥ DMC *mouliné* 743
⑦ DMC *mouliné* 3812
⑧ DMC *mouliné* 956

**Back stitch**

❶ DMC *mouliné* 839
❷ DMC *mouliné* 310
❸ DMC *mouliné* 645
❹ DMC *mouliné* 310
(All black lines)

# VENDING MACHINE

Page 92

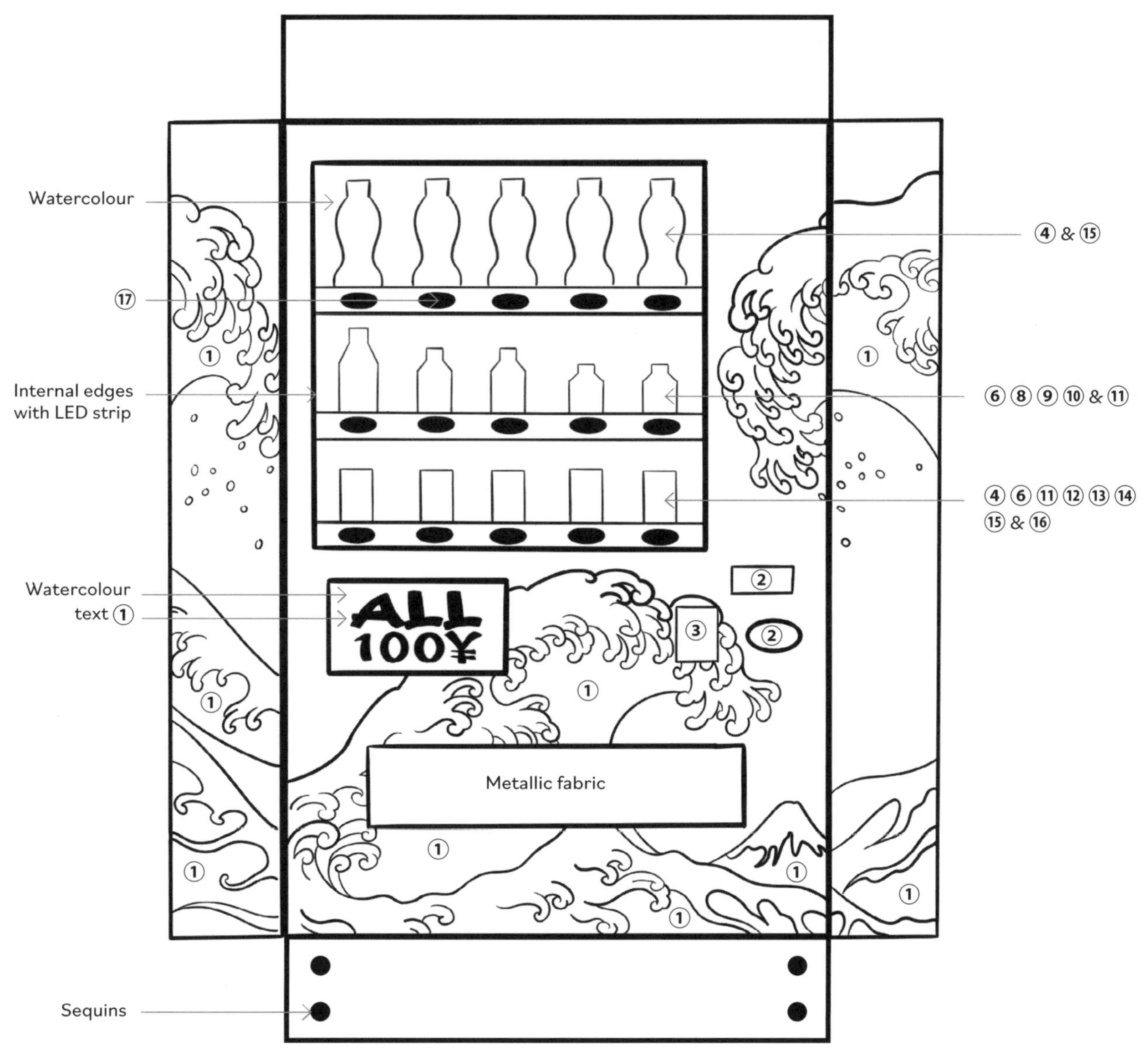


**Satin stitch**

① DMC *mouliné* 517
② DMC *mouliné* 28
③ DMC *mouliné* 645
④ DMC *mouliné* 349
⑤ DMC *mouliné* 433
⑥ DMC *mouliné Blanc*
⑦ DMC *mouliné* 369
⑧ DMC *mouliné* 702
⑨ DMC *mouliné* 369
⑩ DMC *mouliné* 3756
⑪ DMC *mouliné* 742
⑫ DMC *mouliné* 744
⑬ DMC *mouliné* 605
⑭ DMC *mouliné* 25
⑮ DMC *mouliné* 433
⑯ DMC *mouliné* 210
⑰ DMC *étoile* C820

**Back stitch**

❶ DMC *mouliné* 517
(All blue lines)

# KOI FISH

Page 98

**Koi fish spots:** ① & ②

**Satin stitch**

① DMC *mouliné* 900
② DMC *mouliné* 310
③ DMC *mouliné Blanc*
④ DMC *mouliné* 3052

# TAKESHITA STREET

Page 104

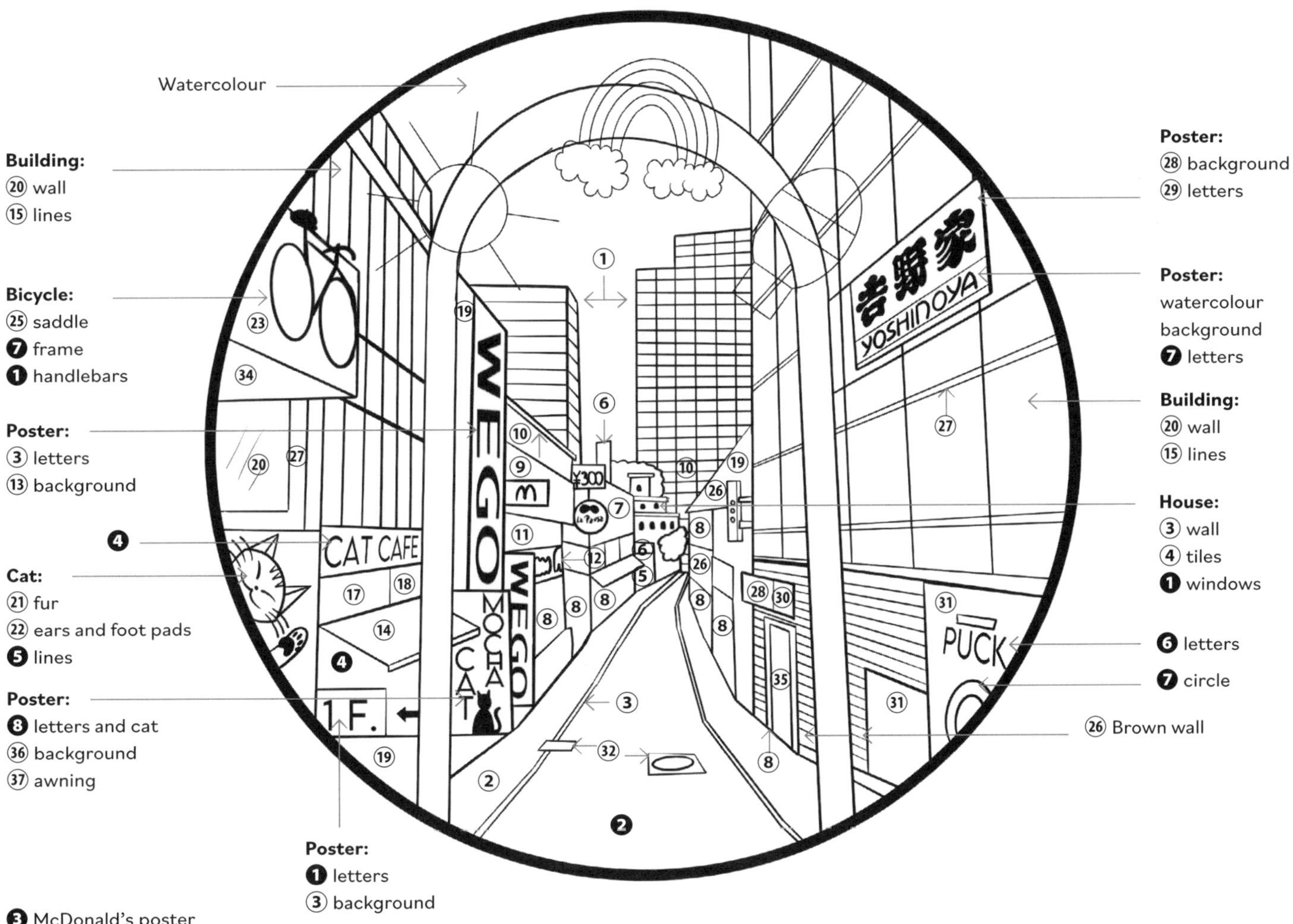


**Satin stitch**

① DMC *mouliné* 3
② DMC *mouliné* 2
③ DMC *mouliné Blanc*
④ DMC *mouliné* 434
⑤ DMC *mouliné* 931
⑥ DMC *mouliné* 894
⑦ DMC *mouliné* 3713
⑧ DMC *mouliné* 744
⑨ DMC *mouliné* 967
⑩ DMC *mouliné* 844
⑪ DMC *mouliné* 780
⑫ DMC *mouliné* 307
⑬ DMC *mouliné* 816
⑭ DMC *mouliné* 340
⑮ DMC *mouliné* 452
⑯ DMC *mouliné* 310
⑰ DMC *mouliné* 3733
⑱ DMC *mouliné* 151
⑲ DMC *mouliné* 25
⑳ DMC *mouliné* 162
㉑ DMC *mouliné* 3854
㉒ DMC *mouliné* 3716
㉓ DMC *mouliné* 312
㉔ DMC *mouliné* 931
㉕ DMC *mouliné* 834
㉖ DMC *mouliné* 3064
㉗ DMC *mouliné* 648
㉘ DMC *mouliné* 720
㉙ DMC *mouliné* 4231
㉚ DMC *mouliné* 838
㉛ DMC *mouliné* 9
㉜ DMC *mouliné* 169
㉝ DMC *mouliné* S415
㉞ DMC *mouliné* 823
㉟ DMC *mouliné* 307
㊱ DMC *mouliné* 307
㊲ DMC *mouliné* 209

**Back stitch**

❶ DMC *mouliné* 310 (All black lines)
❷ DMC *mouliné* 152
❸ DMC *mouliné* 307
❹ DMC *mouliné* 722
❺ DMC *mouliné* 838
❻ DMC *mouliné* 11
❼ DMC *mouliné Blanc*
❽ DMC *mouliné* 3854

**For the felting**

Clover natural wool roving 7920

# INDEX